I'm Too Blessed to be Depressed

Joanna Campbell-Slan

Note to Readers. This book is intended to help situational depression and is not intended as a replacement for medical treatment of clinical depression.

Acknowledgements. Thanks to the sales team at F&W Publications for being guardian angels to this book. Also thanks to yoga queen Dana Nellen for reshaping the editorial and to Matt Piskulic at VIP Graphics and Elaine Floyd at EFG for lighting up the cover and the inside.

Limit of Liability & Disclaimer. The author and publisher have used their best efforts in preparing this book. The author and publisher make no warranty of any kind, expressed or implied, with regard to the instructions and suggestions contained in this book.

Cover & Interior Design: VIP Graphics, St. Louis; (314) 535-1117

I'm Too Blessed to Be Depressed: Stories and guided gratitude journal to move you from stressed to blessed in 30 days.

First Edition. Printed and bound in the United States of America.
04 03 02 01 00   5 4 3 2 1

Library of Congress Catalog Card Number: 00-112089
ISBN: 1-930500-04-1

Published by:
EFG, Inc. • St. Louis, MO
blessed2000@aol.com • www.scrapbookstorytelling.com

Distributed to the trade by:
Writer's Digest Books
An imprint of F&W Publications
1507 Dana Ave., Cincinnati, OH 45207
(800) 289-0963; fax: (513) 531-4082

To my son, Michael Harrison Slan

*I prayed that I might have a child
so I could teach him all that I had learned.*

God heard my prayer and sent me a teacher.

Contents

30 Days from Stressed to Blessed!

Contents

Welcome

 I've been a professional speaker for over ten years, and a listener my whole life. Stories about women have always fascinated me, perhaps because I grew up with two sisters in a family of strong women. I've always shared from the speaking platform the stories of women who have touched my life.

The idea for this book came about rather suddenly when I was flying to Australia a few years ago. The plane hit strong turbulence and I awoke from a deep sleep with one thought: What if I die? What will happen to these stories?

We live in a culture that rarely honors women—those everyday women who are not captains of industry, Fortune 500 company owners or world leaders. We do not honor everyday women or their stories or struggles, and yet these are the women who have and hold babies, love men, and give of themselves to make the lives of others worthwhile. My urge to tell these stories has become overwhelming. By writing these stories down, they can be saved.

These are the stories of heart, soul and passion. You told them to me. I honored them, changed your name for your privacy and now I'm giving them to the world.

You'll notice that I have kept direct and specific religious references to a minimum. I have prayed at churches, synagogues, and temples and many places in between. God never has trouble finding us. We sometimes have trouble finding God.

After each story, you'll see an illuminated blessing from each situation. These are intended to keep us from being caught up in

Welcome

life's minutia. They are an invitation to look beyond surface appearances. After all, everything that happens brings with it a blessing, and our responsibility is to maintain a positive focus so we can incorporate that blessing into our lives.

I have added guided journaling exercises. By trying these new ideas, I hope you will get into the habit of feeling more blessed and less depressed. These aren't here to make you feel more pressured or inadequate. Instead, these guided journaling prompts are designed to help you work your way through stress.

For me, there's a difference between cognitive understanding ("Oh, yeah, that's where I went astray") and feeling at ease with a situation ("Been here, done this, let's move on"). Here I've tried to give you steps to guide you through the process. Since this book's first publication, I've received calls and letters from groups who use the book as a discussion starter. I hope the guided journaling will further enrich those discussions with an opportunity for new insights.

Your stories have given me hope, courage and joy. Your ability to see the good, to make life work, and to give love has been a great blessing to our society.

Thank you for teaching me that I'm too blessed to be depressed. And please, pass it on... share a story with a friend who needs a lift.

Joanna

Joanna Slan
St. Louis, Missouri

Daily Life

Daily Life

Day 1
An Oasis of Tranquility

"The inner belt is backed up all the way downtown," the radio announcer's voice droned.

Christine slammed her fist against the steering wheel. She hated her commute home. The afternoon fight on the expressway had turned her dream job into a nightmare. By the time she pulled into her driveway, she was always tense and angry.

Her family had learned to skulk off the moment they heard the garage door open. Watching them scatter like leaves before a storm made Christine feel even worse! But, what could she do?

"Oh, grrrrrrr—" she had been nosed out of her lane as she was daydreaming. Now, she wouldn't get home for another thirty-five minutes at least. She followed the ramp slowly and found herself sitting at the entrance to the mall.

"Fate..." she muttered and she phoned home to say she wouldn't be home in time for dinner.

The restaurant hostess wrote down her name and informed Christine that a table would be ready in forty-five minutes. For a moment, Christine considered saying, "Forget it!" but it dawned on her that she wouldn't have much better luck anywhere else. So, she smiled meekly and walked off down the mall.

Daily Life

There was a certain sense of freedom about this excursion. She had forty-five minutes to waste, squander, and fritter away.

In one store, she sampled perfumes. The vanilla candles smelled so delicious that she bought one on the spot. Another store piped in the most glorious, relaxing music played over a sound track of whale calls. It was wonderfully soothing. In the third store, she saw a wicker picnic basket with leather buckles. The basket was filled with a display of nonalcoholic beverages, cheeses, and breads. The sign above the basket read, "You don't have to be outside to make it a picnic!"

She stopped. She stared. Why not? Why not transform the inside of her car? She could turn her commute into a sacred space! Quickly, she purchased the basket, the drinks, the cheese and a loaf of French bread. She raced back to buy the whale tape. On the way to the restaurant, she spotted a display of white, damask napkins. She bought two.

The next day, she packed her picnic basket for the return trip home. She put a mini-ice chest of foam inside to keep the cheese and drinks cool. She didn't allow herself to play the tape. She put the scented candle, unlit, in her extra cup holder.

At 5:30 p.m., Christine opened her carbonated fruit seltzer. She flicked open the white damask napkin and centered it in her lap. She popped a slice of cheese into her mouth and bit off a chunk of bread. From the stereo speakers in the back came the lonely cry of a whale. As the other drivers gestured at each other in anger, Christine relaxed for the first time that day.

Daily Life

BLESSING

We have control over our environment.
With proper planning, we can turn any activity
into a joyful celebration of life.

1) *Name a recurring stressful time in your daily life.*

_____
_____
_____
_____
_____
_____
_____
_____
_____

2) *What could you do to change the dynamics of that time?*

❏ _____
❏ _____
❏ _____
❏ _____
❏ _____
❏ _____
❏ _____
❏ _____

Daily Life

3) What materials might you need? Create a shopping list.

❑ _____

❑ _____

❑ _____

❑ _____

❑ _____

❑ _____

❑ _____

❑ _____

4) Who might have ideas you could use for better coping with this time of stress?

_____

_____

_____

_____

_____

_____

5) What is the smallest step you might take TODAY toward changing your time of stress to an oasis of tranquility?

_____

_____

_____

_____

_____

Daily Life

Day 2
Moving On

The smell from the toaster caught Jan's attention before the smoke alarm went off. She ran frantically from one window to another throwing each one open. Then she grabbed the toaster and raced out into the garage. The alarm continued to shriek as she fanned the door back and forth, trying to get as much fresh air into the kitchen as possible.

From the corner of her eye, she saw Bob stroll into the kitchen. He was adjusting his tie with such total disregard for the commotion that she wanted to thump him.

"Toaster again?"

Jan grimaced. "Okay, okay. I hate to spend the money on a new one. If you stand over it, it's really not so bad."

Bob smiled. "Give it up, babe. That toaster is dead, wrecked and it's not coming back. You need to know when to cut your losses." And with a quick kiss, he walked past her and climbed into his car.

Later, Jan was talking with Marlene on the phone. "...then he came home again late. He'd been drinking; I could tell," said Marlene.

Jan tapped her pen on her desk. Every day this week she had spent at least thirty minutes hearing Marlene Fuller talk about her marriage. The two women had been friends and fellow

Daily Life

design collaborators for three years, but Jan was working hard to get her new design business off the ground. The time spent with Marlene would mean working late again tonight.

"You're the only real woman friend I ever had," explained Marlene.

She needs me, thought Jan, I can't let her down.

"Marlene, I'd want to hear more, but I've got to go to a meeting and—"

"OH." Marlene sniffed. "Call me tonight then."

Jan reached to hang up the phone. Marlene was long distance, but then, friends were worth it. Then she heard Marlene's voice start up again—

"Oh, wait! I almost forgot. There's no way I can do the fabric matches for the Peterson project. I don't have the time to go through all the wallpaper books. Sorry."

Jan sat frozen in her seat. Doing Marlene's part of the office design would add eight more hours of work. Work that would have to be done this evening because this was the only available night she had this week. This was the second time Marlene had been unable to complete her part of the project.

"Don't forget to call me tonight," said Marlene, and she hung up.

Jan called Marlene as she had promised. For forty minutes Marlene went on about her husband's drinking, her in-law problems and her job hunt.

"Why don't you consider joining me in my new business?" asked Jan.

"Huh?" sniffed Marlene, "If I wanted to start a business, I would start one on my own. No offense, but you don't know any more about design than I do."

Jan hung up and began to work her way through the wallpaper books. Her son came into the room and stood behind her chair for a while and then he went away. A wave of guilt swept over Jan. She hadn't spent any time at all with her son or her husband in several days. Suddenly, she felt exhausted and angry. She looked at the stack of notes a courier had delivered from Marlene. She looked at the clock. She thought about her phone bill. She felt as though every drop of energy had been wrung out of her body.

Three days later, the postman delivered this note:

> *Marlene—For many years now, we have enjoyed each other's company. However, I realized today that our lives have taken different paths. I wish you every joy in the future. Goodbye, Jan.*

Sitting on top of the trash can outside Jan's house was the toaster.

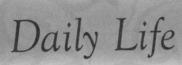

Daily Life

BLESSING

Help me to know when a relationship no longer works for me. Give me the strength to bless the situation and to move on.

1) Quickly write down the names of people you interact with on a daily, weekly and monthly basis.

❑ _____
❑ _____
❑ _____
❑ _____
❑ _____
❑ _____
❑ _____
❑ _____
❑ _____
❑ _____
❑ _____
❑ _____
❑ _____
❑ _____
❑ _____
❑ _____
❑ _____

Daily Life

2) Close your eyes and do a mental review of your relationships. As you revisit each relationship, make notes about the feelings your body contributes.

_____

_____

_____

_____

_____

_____

_____

_____

_____

_____

_____

3) Which relationships bring on feelings of distress?

❑ _____

❑ _____

❑ _____

❑ _____

❑ _____

Daily Life

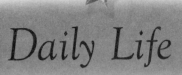

4) *Carefully consider the relationships that bring on distressful feelings. Review and write down what you have learned. Be thankful for the relationship.*

_____

_____

_____

_____

_____

_____

_____

_____

_____

_____

_____

_____

_____

_____

5) *Write a blessing for what the situation has taught you.*

BLESSING: _____

_____

_____

_____

_____

_____

_____

Daily Life

6) *Decide how to move on. List a few ways to become disengaged or to limit the amount of energy the relationship takes.*

_____

_____

_____

_____

_____

_____

_____

_____

_____

_____

_____

_____

_____

WAYS TO DISENGAGE:

❑ _____

_____

❑ _____

_____

❑ _____

_____

❑ _____

_____

Daily Life

7) Write down your new approach to the relationship. Add a note to the other person or people involved, even if you plan to never share that note.

_____

_____

_____

_____

_____

_____

_____

_____

_____

_____

_____

_____

_____

_____

NOTE: _____

_____

_____

_____

_____

_____

_____

Daily Life

Day 3
The High Cost of Affluence

- ✔ Move winter clothes to spare bedroom closet
- ✔ Polish brass sink in den
- ✔ Choose flowers for area around mailbox
- ✔ Oil change for car
- ✔ Buy new bestseller by Sandra Brown
- ✔ Take steaks out of freezer
- ✔ Pick up dog from groomer

Jessica crossed off all the items on her to-do list and checked her wristwatch. Just enough time to drive to the mall for her nail appointment, she noted. While she was there, she would pick up a new copy of *TV Guide* and a tube of body lotion in her favorite fragrance, Ocean Dream.

The CD player in her Lexus kicked in with a jazzy little tune as she flew down the back roads, past the construction sites of other new homes.

"What a drag," she muttered to herself. Her days were filled with endless to-do lists. Then at 3:30 in the afternoon, she was off to pick up Robbie from the private school he attended on the other side of the highway. After taking him to soccer and fixing dinner, she'd work on invitations for the shower she was giving Marianna, a neighbor whose pregnancy surprised the entire subdivision. Why have another child at age 38? Weren't three boys enough?

Daily Life

A parking space reserved for the mall's Super Shopper Club beckoned her. By purchasing more than $100 a month, Jessica earned access to the closest spots. On rainy days, the choice slots were a real godsend, because Jessica could run in without getting wet.

At the nail salon, she signed in, noting she was two minutes early for her appointment. The salon owner, a congenial man with a perpetual smile on his face waved from his office in the back. Jessica scanned the rows of bent heads of nail technicians, all with the same blue-black hair so typical of the Vietnamese. Finally, over the top of a surgical mask, Mary caught Jessica's glance. "Be with you right away! Soon!" called Mary over the head of her current client.

Trying not to feel annoyed, Jessica grabbed the most recent copy of *Style* magazine from the rack and sat down. "Why make an appointment," she growled to herself under her breath, "if she doesn't keep on schedule?"

Jessica was halfway into an article on the favorite underwear of the stars when Mary walked up. "Ready?" Mary asked.

Mary swiped Jessica's old polish with a cotton soaked in chemicals. Her concentration was broken when the client she had just finished leaned over Jessica to slip her a dollar and say, "Enjoy your trip to Vietnam, Mary."

"You're going back home? How long has it been?" Jessica's friends were a well-traveled group, but no one had ever visited Vietnam. For baby-boomers, the place held too many memories.

"Six years," said Mary, never missing a stroke as she wiped off the old color.

Daily Life

"Wow," said Jessica. "That must be a long trip. And expensive."

"I save all my money for it," said Mary. "Work many hours and weekends."

Jessica looked around at the other patrons and workers in the shop. Almost all the clients were exquisitely coiffed, and although dressed for summer, no one would call their clothes casual. The women wore matched shorts and tops with gold leather belts and sandals, linen slacks and fitted linen vests, and one had on a beautiful knee-length sleeveless dress. The look was totally pulled together. By contrast, the Vietnamese women wore jeans and a variety of blouses. While they looked neat and clean, only two of the young ones looked fashionable. On closer inspection, it was clear that their outfits, while carefully chosen, were not of fine quality fabric or design.

"So what will you tell your family about America? About your clients?" said Jessica, partially serious and partially teasing. "Will you tell them about all the fancy ladies whose nails you fix? All the big diamonds we wear? And all the money we all have?"

Mary's eyes never left the nails she was buffing. "I tell them America has so much money. Big diamonds. Two or three cars for every family. Big, big houses for one family. Eat out all time. Change clothes with weather—whole new clothes for different times of year. Each house has two, three televisions. Go see movies. Buy records and magazines. Spend money on dogs and cats. Get food from big, big grocery store. Drive here and drive there," the young woman continued. "Not like home."

Suddenly Jessica felt ashamed.

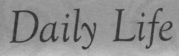

Daily Life

BLESSING

We have so much that we often forget what a privileged life we lead. Help me to remember how fortunate I am.

1) Start a gratitude list. Write down what you are grateful for. Spend at least 10 minutes creating a list. (The time may seem excessive, but it underscores how blessed we all are.)

GRATITUDE LIST

❏ _____
❏ _____
❏ _____
❏ _____
❏ _____
❏ _____
❏ _____
❏ _____
❏ _____
❏ _____
❏ _____
❏ _____
❏ _____
❏ _____
❏ _____
❏ _____
❏ _____

Daily Life

- ❑ _____
- ❑ _____
- ❑ _____
- ❑ _____
- ❑ _____
- ❑ _____
- ❑ _____
- ❑ _____
- ❑ _____
- ❑ _____
- ❑ _____
- ❑ _____

2) Circle the tangible items on your list or make a partial list of items you own, especially those you own in multiples.

- ❑ _____
- ❑ _____
- ❑ _____
- ❑ _____
- ❑ _____
- ❑ _____
- ❑ _____
- ❑ _____
- ❑ _____
- ❑ _____
- ❑ _____

Daily Life

3) How do you feel about what you own? Take a few minutes to journal your reaction to the list of items.

_____
_____
_____
_____
_____
_____
_____
_____
_____
_____
_____
_____

4) Now ask yourself, "Do I own these things or do they own me?"

_____
_____
_____
_____
_____
_____
_____
_____
_____
_____

Daily Life

5) Re-evaluate your ownership. What items are weighing you down? What has increased in number beyond its capacity to give you joy?

_____

_____

_____

_____

_____

_____

_____

_____

_____

6) Make a list of areas you'd like to pare down.

❑ _____

❑ _____

❑ _____

❑ _____

❑ _____

❑ _____

❑ _____

❑ _____

❑ _____

❑ _____

❑ _____

Daily Life

- ☐ _____
- ☐ _____
- ☐ _____
- ☐ _____
- ☐ _____
- ☐ _____
- ☐ _____
- ☐ _____
- ☐ _____
- ☐ _____
- ☐ _____

7) Make an appointment with yourself to take a bag of excess belongings to a charity. Afterwards, write down how you felt about this entire experience.

_____
_____
_____
_____
_____
_____
_____
_____
_____
_____
_____

Daily Life

Day 4
A Lesson in Priorities

In his hand was a fluorescent orange note that Rose happened to snatch before Matt ran out to play with the boy next door.

Dear Moms: Tomorrow at our school we will be working on a project that will eventually be your Mothers Day gifts. Your child will need an empty 8-ounce frozen juice container and a stack of magazines. Thanks!

—Loretta Lowski, Pre-School Instructor.

Rose looked at the note with horror. Before she put Matt to bed this evening she had to pack for a two-day trip, finish a proposal, mail out bills and wash enough of his clothes to last him while she was gone. This was the third time this month that Loretta Lowski had sent home a note and expected her to alter her evening plans to come up with materials for a project. Rose's hands trembled. Dan wouldn't be home until after midnight. The neighbors were out of town. Unless she grabbed Matt, hopped in the car and drove the thirty-minute round trip to the store, no eight-ounce frozen juice can was in sight. Quickly she rinsed out a juice box and picked six magazines from the pile next to her toilet. It would have to do.

Three days later, Rose picked up Matt from pre-school. The two were walking happily down the hallway from his classroom and

Daily Life

toward the door when Rose heard a querulous voice behind her, "Mrs. McKenzie! Mrs. McKenzie!"

Loretta Lowski marched up the hallway pumping both arms like a race walker. "We MUST talk," Loretta hissed. "Do you realize that Matt was the only child in his class who did not have the required materials for his project?" Seeing the blank look on Rose's face, Loretta pressed on adding, "How can he learn to follow instructions if he doesn't have his empty 8-ounce frozen juice container? School is all about discipline, you know. Please try to pay more attention in the future."

With that she turned on her heel and sprinted back down the hallway, arms pumping furiously.

Dear Moms: We are having a fund raising bake sale Friday. We need each of you to provide two dozen home baked goodies, individually wrapped and marked for sale. You must have these at school two hours before school starts. We are not able to store food overnight so please DO NOT send your baked items the night before.

Rose looked at the fluorescent green note and felt sick. She did not bake. She never had time. This week was especially crammed because she had committed months before to help with her association's educational program. Dan would be working late to finish his report on the project he'd headed up at work.

Rose picked up the phone in a panic. "Mrs. Lowski, I apologize for calling you at home, but I can't get this done by tomorrow. Could I make a donation to the school? I do want to help out, but I don't have the time to bake for you, at least not tonight."

Daily Life

A long silence followed. Mrs. Lowski huffed. "Do you realize the impact this will have on your son? Again, Chad will be the only child who does not have the required materials. Do you know how difficult it is to be different?"

Rose swallowed hard. "I think I do know how it feels to be different, Mrs. Lowski. I'm obviously different from all your other mothers."

"Perhaps," said Mrs. Lowski, in a slow and quiet voice, "perhaps what you really want is a day care situation. Being a pre-school, we look for a high level of parental involvement. From what you're telling me, that isn't possible in your situation."

Two weeks later...

Rose picked up Chad and gave him a hug. Then she walked over to Mrs. Lowski. "We need to talk," said Chad's teacher as a tense crease formed between her eyes.

Rose sighed. "Yes, we do. Let's go to the principal's office."

Mrs. White rearranged the papers on her desk and cleared her throat. "How can I help you, ladies?"

Mrs. Lowski began in a low and trembling voice. "As you know, I've been teaching for almost 40 years. I always say that parental involvement is a critical part of the learning process. Children need to know that their needs come first. That the adults in their lives will be there for them. Twice now, poor little Chad has been singled out—been different—because his mother hasn't been able to juggle her work schedule and his needs."

Daily Life

Mrs. White said nothing. "We know how important your methods have been to our school, Mrs. Lowski. Thank you for your input. I'll take it from here."

As Mrs. Lowski walked stiffly out of the office. Rose took a deep breath. She soothed the fabric over her knees. She lifted her eyes to Mrs. White's kindly face. "I'm trying…"

Mrs. White interrupted her. "Yes, dear, of course you are. But perhaps this situation is simply a mismatch. With two years to go until retirement, Mrs. Lowski won't change. Our alumni and donors have grown to expect bake sales and juice can crafts. You, however, are young and flexible. Let's explore our options. Have you looked into our sister school? It's only two years old, and I think you'd like it."

One week later, Chad moved to the sister school. The teacher there was easygoing and cheerful. She encouraged the children to eat granola, not cookies, and she spent her afternoon breaks downstairs in the nursery area visiting her own infant daughter.

Daily Life

BLESSING

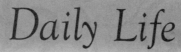

Thank you for the opportunity to find supportive people in my life. When I encounter others who do not understand my lifestyle, remind me that I can move on.

1) *Definition of support person: A person you look to for help or assistance. Divide a piece of paper into halves and label them with a plus sign on one side and a minus on the other. On the plus side list those support people in your life whose presence is beneficial and who make you feel more capable. On the minus side, list those support people who make you feel incompetent.*

+   –

_____

_____

_____

_____

_____

Daily Life

2) *Choose one non-supporting person on your list. Write about the impact of the non-supporting person. Often the lack of support makes your role as a wife, worker or mother more difficult. Is this happening?*

_____

_____

_____

_____

_____

_____

_____

_____

_____

_____

3) *Can this relationship be salvaged? Have you approached the person with your needs and wants before?*

_____

_____

_____

_____

_____

_____

_____

_____

Daily Life

4) *Write a script for what you need to tell this person. Start every sentence with "I." The sentences should explain what you need or want. They will sound like this: "I need to feel you are on my side. I want you to keep your disagreements with my decision to work to yourself." Explain how the lack of support undermines your capability. You might say, "When you criticize my decision to work, you suggest to my child that I am making a mistake."*

_____

_____

_____

_____

_____

_____

_____

_____

_____

_____

5) *Now state the new behavior you request. "In the future, I ask that you do not make disparaging comments about my job."*

_____

_____

_____

_____

_____

_____

_____

Daily Life

6) *Practice your script.*

7) *Tell the support person what you want. Observe his or her reaction and decide what you need to do next.*

Daily Life

Day 5
Pass It On!

Beth waited patiently as the sports utility vehicle backed out of the only parking space available in front of the grocery store. The steady click, click of the windshield wipers kept time with the torrential rain outside her car. She watched as the black behemoth swung into the far right lane. Then she slammed on her brakes as a bright red Lincoln Continental pulled into the space from the other side of the parked cars.

"Well, I'll be danged! You jerk! You idiot!" Beth groaned in disgust. She honked her horn twice but the person in the red car simply slipped out and ran through the rain.

Ten minutes later, Beth found another spot at the far side of the lot. By the time she made it to the automatic doors of the store, Beth was drenched.

She grabbed the only cart left and began to fill it with fruit. She also needed a head of lettuce, but the pale piles of green balls seemed completely picked over. She picked up one after another until she discovered one that felt dense. When she turned to put the greens in her cart, it was no where to be found.

"All we have left are these hand-held baskets," said the teenage checkout boy. Beth took it from him without thanking him.

Again, she picked out fruit. Growing conscious of the basket's weight on her arm, she decided against taking advantage of the sale on canned vegetables. In the dairy department, she slipped

38

Daily Life

on a watery patch on the floor. The bakery was out of whole grain bread. "Looks like it's English muffins for breakfast," she murmured.

In the deli department, two workers struggled to keep up with the crowd of shoppers. "Take a number, puuhhhlezze!" yelled one of them over the heads of the teeming throng. Beth pulled #95 from the machine and glanced up to see they were serving #85. Blocking her view of the case was a woman with two kids, one in the cart and one on her hip. "Cody, which drumstick do you want, honey?" asked the mom. Cody considered, taking his fingers out of his mouth. "Dat one," and he pointed into the case.

"This one?" asked the clerk.

"No."

"This one?"

"No."

"This one?"

Beth couldn't stand it anymore. She walked over to the packaged deli products and bought more potato salad than her family could eat in a week. She grabbed packaged lunch meat, although she could predict her husband's complaints about it.

By the time she made it to the check out line, her shoes were drying and starting to pinch her feet.

"That'll be $25.45," said the big-haired young lady between chomps on her gum. Snapping and twirling it around her finger, she regarded Beth quietly. "And do you know your mascara has run down your cheek?"

Daily Life

Beth didn't care. As she combed through her purse, her gut tied into a knot. Where was her checkbook? Suddenly, she remembered that her husband had balanced it this morning. Odds were good that the checkbook was sitting where he had left it, on the kitchen counter. She opened her wallet. With change she had exactly $24.45.

"You're a dollar short," said the gum-chewer. "What do you want to put back? Or do you want to come back for all this later?"

"Here," said a voice at Beth's elbow. Cody's mother leaned over and handed the clerk a dollar.

Beth turned to face her rescuer. "If you'll write down your address, I'll send you the money."

The woman readjusted the child on her hip as he dribbled pieces of donut down her leg. "Naw," she said, "instead, pass it on. Help somebody else. Lord knows, we all need a little help from time to time."

Daily Life

BLESSING

Help me to reverse the negative spirals I allow myself to get into. Allow me to start the process of kindness. Let me never miss an opportunity to pass it on.

1) For a five-day period, send out a thank you note each day to one person who has made a difference in your life.

DAY 1: _____

DAY 2: _____

DAY 3: _____

DAY 4: _____

DAY 5: _____

2) Review a negative spiral that you experienced recently. Write about what happened. How did the spiral start? What conversation went on in your head?

_____
_____
_____
_____
_____
_____

Daily Life

_____

_____

_____

_____

_____

_____

3) Experiment. Plan to take an entire day helping other people. Actively look for ways to put the needs of others first. You might open doors for others, offer to take on a disliked office task, let other vehicles have the right of way, allow another shopper to go through a check out lane before you or put money in a soon-to-expire meter. Write about your experience.

_____

_____

_____

_____

_____

_____

_____

_____

_____

_____

_____

_____

Daily Life

4) Write about a situation that frustrated you. What was happening? Now give the person or persons in the situation the benefit of the doubt. Write down a logical explanation for their actions that would excuse their behavior. How could you have changed your view of what happened to make it positive?

_____

_____

_____

_____

_____

_____

_____

_____

5) Write a prayer for someone who has annoyed you recently. Pretend you are still in the annoying situation. Here's a sample:

> "Bless and watch over this lady who is driving 10 miles an hour in a 35 mile an hour zone. Help her to feel safe. Help her to get where she's going and back without incident. Help all who come in contact with her to find patience."

_____

_____

_____

_____

_____

_____

_____

Daily Life

Day 6
All My Needs

Charlotte shoved back her chair from the kitchen table and walked out onto her deck. The spring had been gentle that year. Her herb garden was making a tentative appearance through the soft soil. Beyond her yard, rows of corn plants poked up their heads like children waking up from naps. She turned and looked at the house, her dream house. When they moved, she would be giving up a balcony off the master bedroom, a walk-in closet, a marble fireplace, and an oak-paneled library.

"Okay, Dennis. Call the real estate agent. Do it quickly though, before I lose my nerve," she said.

A couple of nights later, over a plate of spaghetti, Dennis tried to comfort her.

"You won't have to pack this time," he said. "The business can pay for it. I got an estimate."

The plate swam before her eyes. Charlotte asked, "How much?"

"They want $5000," said Dennis. "They can't get to us for sixty days. That would mean we have to turn down the offer on the house. The Paulsons want to move in here within the next three weeks." He was trying to sound casual, but she knew how much an extra $5000 would mean to his business. The money would help him keep his creditors at bay while he sold off unprofitable stores and closed branch offices.

Daily Life

Charlotte was torn. Packing. What an awful job, she thought, but I can do it. Besides, why move to help the business if moving actually costs the business. If we don't sell to the Paulsons, we can't move to Kansas City. The longer it takes to move, the more danger we are in of losing the business.

"I'll pack us up," she said.

That night she sipped tea on the deck. The herb garden could be started in the new place. She could dig up starts and nurture them over the summer. She trusted Dennis to turn his company around. No one worked harder or knew more than he. But the real loss would be...petunias.

Each summer Charlotte had planted huge clay pots of petunias. Riotous, colorful, fragrant petunias lined her deck. Each night of summer, she and Dennis would sit for a while in the growing dark and enjoy their heady scent. This summer, planting the petunias would be ridiculous. There would be no time. Moving all the planted pots would be impossible. Charlotte emptied her tea cup over the rail into an empty pot and went back inside. Outside the pots lined up like squatting soldiers in an army camp.

For the next few weeks, Charlotte packed. Spending $300 on boxes, unprinted newspaper, and tape, she was as well-equipped as the local moving company. In between wrapping and packing, she answered calls from the real estate agent.

"Could I slip in and take measurements for the Paulsons?" was the request one week. The next week the agent needed photos so the Paulsons could buy window treatments. The third week

Daily Life

Charlotte alternately packed and dodged an interior decorator making quick notes on a clipboard and glowering at Charlotte and Dennis's choice of furniture.

With each passing day, Charlotte added a new strained muscle or paper cut to her aching body. After dinner, she bypassed the deck and continued the long job of wrapping and packing all their belongings. Instinctively, she avoided reminding herself of the lost petunias.

The morning of the move dawned far too early as the alarm clock rang with fervor. Charlotte threw on old clothes, a little makeup and ran downstairs to grab a bowl of cereal.

The deck seemed to call to her. Why not? How could it possibly hurt to say goodbye? She quickly made a cup of peppermint tea and stepped onto the rough cedar floor. Then she stopped in her tracks. There in front of her was a bright blaze of color, a pot filled with racy red petunias.

But that's impossible! Charlotte said to herself. Commercially grown petunias are usually hybrids that won't reproduce from year to year! How could this have happened?

With a joyous gesture, she bent her head to the flower and took a long slow breath of petunia.

Daily Life

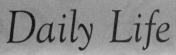

BLESSING

Heavenly Creator, you know my every need. Thank you for loving me and caring for me so completely.

1) Write down what you need right now.

_____

_____

_____

_____

_____

_____

_____

_____

2) Make a list of those items, rituals and sayings that give you comfort.

❏ _____

❏ _____

❏ _____

❏ _____

❏ _____

❏ _____

❏ _____

❏ _____

Daily Life

3) Write down a plan for a perfect hour. Where would you be? What would you eat or drink? What clothes would you wear? What would you do? Who would you want as company? Be as detailed as possible.

_____

_____

_____

_____

_____

_____

_____

_____

_____

_____

_____

_____

_____

_____

_____

_____

_____

_____

_____

_____

_____

_____

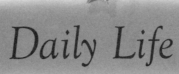

Daily Life

4) Consider what it is about certain items, rituals and sayings that comfort you. Write down a saying that gives you comfort.

For example, the saying "Nothing can keep God's good from me" reminds me that even when circumstances look bleak, God is in control. This saying teaches me to look beyond the superficial aspects of life.

_____

_____

_____

_____

_____

_____

_____

_____

_____

_____

_____

_____

_____

5) Plan to add one item to your life that would help you feel more satisfied.

_____

_____

_____

_____

Family

Family

Day 7
Flea Bites

The number you have reached is no longer in service..." Rita shook her head. Her mother's phone *was* in service. It was *her* phone that didn't work.

For three months, the Clarks had been nursing a failing phone. It skipped numbers, disconnected mid-conversation and hummed wildly for no apparent reason. Since Rita made most of her calls from the family kitchen, tucking the phone under her ear as she scurried to cook and set the table, Rita had complained steadily to Steve about the problem.

"Aw, hon, you're just oversensitive," he laughed in that good natured way of his. "It always works for me." Maybe it does, thought Rita, but that doesn't help me one bit. She pulled the casserole out of the oven and stirred furiously.

"Ma! Did you remember to move my piano lesson?" Connie asked, looking up from her homework.

Rita sighed and shook her head. She removed a head of lettuce from the refrigerator and, balancing the lettuce in one hand and the phone in the other, she dialed the piano teacher's house.

"Hello," Mrs. Gill answered like the cheery octogenarian she was. Her voice held the remnants of old money and culture. Rita quickly explained her plight, tearing lettuce into bite-sized chunks as she talked.

"Of course, we can move the lesson. One must, however, consult one's date book first to be clear about commitments—"

Family

"YEEEOOWW! Shhh—" and with a stunned jerk, Rita dropped the phone. It had stung her. She put her hand to her throbbing temple and tentatively picked up the receiver from the floor.

"Well, I never," began an indignant Mrs. Gill. Rita slumped into the kitchen chair. Her head hurt so badly she could barely focus. "Mrs. Gill, the phone stung me. I mean, it bit me! I mean, my head hurts so badly that I think I may be sick."

After dinner, Rita took the dog for a walk. Her head still hurt. Steve had heard the story from Connie and had shaken his head in disbelief. As Rita stepped into the garage, she felt a new wave of frustration. Surrounding her were conveniences: two cars, a freezer, a snow blower, a lawn mower and electric hedge clippers. On his work bench was Steve's belt sander and tools. All ready to serve...

She turned on her heel and marched back into the kitchen. She yanked the phone from the wall. She closed the garage door behind her and put the phone in the middle of Steve' work space. She pulled his safety glasses over her eyes. She picked up his sledge hammer and beat the phone into tiny pieces of plastic and wire. She swept up the pieces and threw them in the trash. The dog sat beside the back door and waited patiently for her to finish her chore. Then they went for a walk.

"How was your walk, sweetheart?" asked Steve when she returned.

"It was," said Rita, "very freeing."

53

Family

BLESSING

My life is filled with gadgets designed to add to my convenience. When they cease to be a convenience and start to be an irritation, I can make new choices. I am blessed to be free to clear small irritations from my life.

1) List objects in your life that don't work the way they should. Be sure to include clothes that don't fit quite right.

❏ _____
❏ _____
❏ _____
❏ _____
❏ _____
❏ _____
❏ _____
❏ _____
❏ _____
❏ _____
❏ _____
❏ _____
❏ _____
❏ _____
❏ _____
❏ _____
❏ _____
❏ _____

Family

2) Journal about how these objects make you feel. Do they pull your energy down? Leave you feeling less confident? Do they cause you to feel frazzled?

_____

_____

_____

_____

_____

_____

_____

_____

_____

_____

_____

_____

_____

_____

_____

_____

_____

3) Plan to get rid of at least two of the objects.

❏ _____

❏ _____

Family

4) Work out on paper how you'll live without those objects. Will they need to be replaced? If so, what steps must you take to replace them?

_____

_____

_____

_____

_____

_____

_____

_____

_____

5) Get rid of the offenders. Write about how you felt when you told these ineffective objects "goodbye."

_____

_____

_____

_____

_____

_____

_____

_____

_____

Family

Day 8
An International Flavor

Claire scratched "soup" off her grocery list. Standing in front of the display of red and white cans, she let her mind wander. Should she buy the plain tomato? Or the Italian tomato? Did it matter?

With Jeff back in school, every penny counted. He was zipping his way through the special program that would prepare him for certification as an echocardiography specialist. Already, he'd had two nibbles on jobs, thanks in part to the prestige of the school he was attending and in part to hearty recommendations from his teachers.

"They say I'm a natural at this," he said as he ran a hand through his shoulder length auburn hair. "Thank goodness. I was beginning to wonder if I'd ever find my niche!"

So had she. Not that she had ever lost faith in Jeff. She loved him and knew him to be a talented and steady worker. But, it had taken him a long time to settle on a career path. As a result, their earnings had bounced up and down for several years. Now, with him back in school, money was tight. Soup and sandwiches for dinner were the norm. Eating out was postponed until later, after graduation.

The economizing had taken a toll on their lives. By nature, she and Jeff were social animals. The penny-pinching was getting to her, and although she tried to stay "up" she felt herself short-tempered as she served yet another meal of low cost fare.

Family

Back to the business at hand, she thought, studying the label of the Italian soup. Oh, to be in Italy, she sighed. To eat bruschetta, tomatoes sprinkled with basil, and....

Why not? Even if they couldn't visit Italy, they could eat as though they were there. She grabbed the can of Italian tomato soup, and then she turned her cart back toward the bakery department. There she grabbed a long loaf of French bread and a round loaf of focaccia. From the cheeses, she selected a small slice of brie that she could heat in the oven. From the produce department, she chose several ripe pears in shades of green, gold and burnished red.

On the way home, she stopped by the library. She borrowed two books of art and a CD of classical music.

When Jeff walked through the front door, he was greeted by an aria from an Italian opera. On the low coffee table three candles sat lit with flames that wavered in the mirror beneath them. From the kitchen came the delectable odor of cheese. "Ciao!" said Claire, peeping around the doorway.

Thus began the first of their International Nights. Claire and Jeff would look through cookbooks and choose simple fare from around the world. Every Wednesday, they would decorate in their version of some international locale. Local music added to the ambience.

Although the dinners began as a way around a meager budget, today they still enjoy their international holidays. "We travel the world," they'll tell you, "from right here in our home."

Family

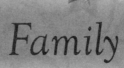

BLESSING

I don't need a lot of money to enjoy my life. Help me to use my creativity to experience the life I want.

1) Make a list of countries, states or regions you would like to visit. Or, list things you love but can't afford right now. Circle three or four that seem particularly appealing.

- ❏ _____
- ❏ _____
- ❏ _____
- ❏ _____
- ❏ _____
- ❏ _____
- ❏ _____
- ❏ _____
- ❏ _____
- ❏ _____
- ❏ _____
- ❏ _____
- ❏ _____
- ❏ _____
- ❏ _____
- ❏ _____
- ❏ _____
- ❏ _____

Family

2) Take your shortened list with you to the library. Find a cookbook with recipes from an area you'd like to visit. Find music and a travel book from that area. Write down the recipe you want to make along with any side dishes you'd like to try.

 ## RECIPE

 ## RECIPE

Family

3) Make the food purchases you need to create your international cuisine. While you make (or even while you defrost) the food, make a note to yourself about the colors, texture and smell of the food. Often different areas rely on different spices or preparation. Note how this area is different from what you are accustomed to.

_____

_____

_____

_____

_____

_____

_____

_____

_____

_____

4) Put on music and enjoy your meal. Look through the travel book. Note next to your recipe if you liked the food or if you'd make the dish again with adjustments.

5) Choose your next culinary visit and write down where you will go.

THE NEXT STOP IS: _____

_____

_____

Family

Day 9
Permission Granted

The small figure slipped off the sofa and onto the floor. A few inches at a time, Molly scooted closer to the TV. Her head full of fluffy blonde curls leaned nearer and nearer to the screen.

"That's too close!" yelled her dad from across the room. He peered over the top of his newspaper and caught her eye.

"But I can't see," wailed the seven-year-old.

Emily held her tongue. They went through this battle every night. Molly complained she couldn't see and Scott fussed at her for being too close. The words on the tip of her tongue were swallowed with great effort. *She needs glasses.* Scott and Emily had gone 'round and 'round about the subject. As much as she loved him, Scott Carson had his faults. His bullheadedness was the worst of them. For such a kind man, he could be intractable. Once he made up his mind about something—anything!—Scott considered backing down impossible. Typically, Emily shrugged her shoulders and let him have his way. But now and again, the situation grew more and more tense. She hated to see her husband and daughter upset with each other. She also hated the stopped up sink that Scott swore was only "slow to drain," and the broken radio in her car that he "would get to" and the pile of caps on the floor of their closet that he claimed, "There's no way to organize."

Later that evening, Emily and her neighbor Sue went for their customary walk around the neighborhood.

Family

"He's driving me nuts," said Emily, struggling to keep up with the pace set by long-legged Sue. "I can handle messes he procrastinates on tackling, but this isn't fair to Molly."

Sue dodged a crack in the sidewalk. "Emily, handle it and move on."

Standing in the shower that night, Emily felt a wave of sadness. As the water poured on her head, she reviewed her conversation with Sue. She was always there for Sue, emotionally. Didn't she always listen to Sue's problems? How dare she cut off Emily's complaints with an abrupt, "Handle it and move on!" The stinging of the water prickled Emily's back. She wasn't even sure what Sue had meant. How could she handle situations if Scott said, "No"? What would happen?

The next morning Emily's phone rang an hour before lunch. "Molly's complaining of a headache, and we have her here in the office lying down," said the school nurse. "We've noticed her headaches are becoming more and more frequent. Have you had her eyes checked recently?"

Emily felt her face flush with embarrassment. She was not about to say her husband wouldn't let her. Instead, she answered, "I'll make an appointment today."

Thanks to a timely cancellation, Emily was able to pick up Molly later that afternoon and get right into the optometrist's office at the mall. The doctor flashed the eye chart on the wall and asked Molly to read. A long silence followed. An hour later they chose a set of frames for Molly. After another hour of wandering around in the mall, Molly walked in and was fitted for her new pair of glasses. The girl skipped merrily along the mall corridor reading signs out loud.

Family

Why didn't I do this before? Emily asked herself. *Look at what I put her through.*

That evening Scott inspected his daughter's new glasses. "Try to read the words on the television without them," he asked. "Now with them," he said more quietly. Their daughter sat on the sofa and read the special offer on television for the first time. "Well, I'll be jiggered," he whispered.

The next day Emily made an appointment to have her car radio fixed. She called the plumber and set up a time for him to unstop the drain. Then, she drove to the store and bought a plastic rack made for storing men's caps. Before she picked up Molly from school, she stopped at a little coffee shop she'd been pestering Scott to visit with her. He hated fancy coffee. She bought two small bags—Almond Mocha and Hazelnut— after sampling them.

"But I don't like this stuff," said Scott when he noticed it on the kitchen counter.

Emily smiled at him. "You don't have to drink it, honey."

"But why did you buy it?" he sputtered.

She gave him her most tolerant look. "Honey... get over it."

Family

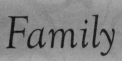

BLESSING

Give me the strength to take action instead of whining. Help me to move ahead without anger or sarcasm. Teach me to take care of my needs without waiting for others to approve.

1) Consider a situation where you are not being given permission by another to act as you think best. Jot down that situation.

_____

_____

_____

_____

_____

_____

_____

_____

_____

2) Write down the stresses or inconveniences you experience because you are giving up your control.

_____

_____

_____

_____

_____

_____

Family

3) How does this impact your relationship with the other person?

_____

_____

_____

_____

_____

_____

_____

_____

_____

_____

4) Imagine yourself in this situation or in similar situations. What is it you want? Write down at least five endings to this sentence: "I want..."

1: _____

_____

2: _____

_____

3: _____

_____

4: _____

_____

5: _____

_____

Family

5) Remembering not to explain, bargain or blame, write down how you plan to take more control over a particular situation in the future.

_____

_____

_____

_____

_____

_____

_____

_____

_____

6) When you take control, make a journal note about how it felt and the other person's reaction. (Often we imagine a huge problem and there isn't one.)

_____

_____

_____

_____

_____

_____

_____

Family

Day 10
Getting Real

"Happy Birthday!" Elmer Nash looked around with an expression of shock on his face. Then the large man slowly began to smile.

Angie Nash yelled from the back of the crowd, "Smile!" And the big man turned to the sound of her voice, but when he caught sight of her, he frowned slightly.

Angie waited for his smile to return and then took the picture. As she stepped down from the chair, and advanced the film, she turned her back on the happy family group. She blinked rapidly to avoid letting tears spill down her face. After seven years of marriage to Joe, she was still an outsider to his family. Angie's own parents had died when she was in high school. She had married into the Nash clan with dreams of finding a new family. But old Elmer Nash didn't like her.

"I cain't take a shine to her, Joe," said Elmer. "Now that Patricia Stevens you brought home was a real doll. Are you sure you got the right girl?" Elmer was accustomed to having his word obeyed as law. He had handpicked his other two daughters-in-law, and he had helped one of them, Liz, get a job. Elmer was used to being the king of all he surveyed. When Joe refused to dump Angie, Elmer pouted. "She'll never fit in," he grumbled. "She don't bring enough to the marriage."

"It's like this," Elmer's wife, Doris, explained. "Joe owes his father respect. Elmer thinks that Joe was disrespectful when he married you. I expect he'll get over it, but he sure isn't happy."

Family

Angie wiped her eyes and stepped to the bright picture window, bordered by exotic plants with blooms of bright red. They drooped in the early evening summer sun. Angie knew how they felt. Doris had thought the old man would come around. But he hadn't. No matter how much Angie tried, Elmer kept his distance. Often, like today, he would stare at her as if to say, "Why are you here?"

Yet Angie kept trying. She was the one who had planned his surprise 65th birthday party, renting his favorite restaurant, Come On Inn, ordering the cake and his favorite foods, inviting his best friends from the railroad yard. Maybe when Elmer Nash found out who was responsible, he would finally realize the depth of Angie's desire to be a part of his family.

She gathered her purse, the disposable camera she bought for this day, and sat down next to her husband. Elmer sat across from her. Time and time again friends came over to shake his hand and wish him well. After dinner, Elmer blew out the candles on his yellow cake, iced with vanilla frosting and sprinkled—as he liked it—with coconut. He had spoken to every person in the room but Angie. To keep from dwelling on her embarrassment, Angie looked past her father-in-law and out the picture window where a border of bright flowers edged the sidewalk.

That's when she saw the hummingbird. Emerald green and as long as her thumb, he balanced in the air with his tail fanned out beneath him. He moved up and down the plate glass window, trying to get to the plastic flowers inside. First, he zigged to the right. Then, he darted to the left. Below him was a feast of real flowers, but he concentrated all his efforts on the gaudy plastic behind the glass. For the better part of five minutes, the tiny bird wore himself out moving from side to side.

Family

Angie realized that while the bird was in no danger, he was wearing himself out. "Look around!" she wanted to shout, "Your efforts are better spent somewhere else! Those flowers aren't even real."

Joe's voice broke through her reverie. "Dad, Angie is the one who put this whole party together," said Joe proudly. "She spent a lot of time on this for you."

Elmer had been talking to Bitsy when Joe made his announcement. Uneasily, he tore his glaze from Bitsy's face to look at Angie. "Thanks," he grunted. Then he turned back to Bitsy and asked her a question about her work.

I am the hummingbird, thought Angie, I keep spending energy trying to break through a plate glass window to get to what? Plastic flowers!

Angie and Joe had a long talk that evening. "I am no longer willing to give your father so much of my time and energy," said Angie. "He's made it clear that he doesn't approve of me. I support you in your visits, and I'll go every once in a while, but I won't make a habit of it. And, from now on you are responsible for your family's birthdays and significant dates. I'll take care of those for my family."

Since then, Joe and Angie rarely visit the older Nash's home together. Angie is polite to Elmer, but she doesn't make any

Family

special effort to please him. Joe forgot Elmer's birthday the next year, and when Doris and Elmer fussed about it, Joe took responsibility. A week later, Elmer called and asked to speak to Angie. "Why don't you visit anymore? Why don't you take care of our gifts and such?"

Angie took a deep breath and said, "Let's be honest, Elmer. You don't like me. You never have. I respect you as Joe's dad, but there's no reason for me to be around you. I encourage Joe to spend time with you. I do show up for major holidays. Since you don't care for me, I think it's probably easier for both of us." There was a stunned silence on the other end of the phone.

Angie waited long enough to be polite and then finished the conversation, "Good-bye, Elmer."

Family

BLESSING

Teach me to accept people and circumstances I can't change. Help me to know when I am shut out by a glass window. Give me the grace to move on without anger.

1) Make note of a recurring unpleasant situation in your life.

_____

_____

_____

_____

_____

_____

_____

2) Write down your response to the question, "Is this situation likely to change?" If the answer is no, you need to decide how **you** must change.

_____

_____

_____

_____

_____

_____

_____

_____

Family

3) *Determine what is the least level of involvement you could have in your troublesome situation. For example, if you always have problems with your brother, how infrequently could you visit or correspond? If you always have problems with your child's teacher, could you ask your spouse to do most of the communicating?*

_____

_____

_____

_____

_____

_____

_____

4) *Think of what you are learning from this experience. Without being too hard on yourself or giving in to pity, try to journal what good you can take from this.*

_____

_____

_____

_____

_____

_____

_____

_____

_____

Family

5) Write a script that explains your new position. Re-write the script until it is honest and not inflammatory. Prepare a direct response to the direct question, "What's happening here?" Remember: Your goal is not to blame. Your goal is to accept what can't be changed at this moment in time while protecting yourself from the negative feelings of others.

_____

_____

_____

_____

_____

_____

_____

_____

_____

_____

_____

_____

_____

_____

_____

_____

_____

Family

Day 11
The Ruby and Pearl Ring

The three rings glittered in their mother's hand. "Since you are the oldest, Hannah, you can choose first."

Hannah, Miriam, and Rachel sat in a row on the edge of their mother's bed. One ring was twin diamonds, one was a pearl surrounded by tiny diamonds, and the last ring was an ornate Victorian confection of a ruby surrounded by pearls.

Hannah paused. All the girls wanted the ruby and pearl ring. For years now, when they were sick and at home from school, Mom had entertained them by opening her mother's jewelry box and letting them ooh and ahh over the contents. The ruby and pearl ring was exactly what a fairy tale princess might wear. Her sisters wanted it, too. But, she was the oldest and Mom had set the ground rules.

"I'll take the ruby and pearl ring," she said, trying hard to keep the triumph out of her voice. Her younger sisters sullenly made their choices. Mom put Rachel's pearl and diamond ring back in the jewelry box to give her when she turned sixteen. Miriam promised not to wear the twin diamond ring except for special occasions.

"Lucky you," whined Rachel as she passed Hannah in the long hallway.

"Look," said Hannah abruptly, "Miriam, come here, too. One of us had to get it and the other two would have been angry no

Family

matter what. So, cool it. These rings aren't worth fighting over, are they? After all, we're sisters." The two younger girls rolled their eyes, sighed and nodded.

"Yeh," said Miriam. "I guess you're right. But—if you die, leave me that ring!"

"No, me!" shouted Rachel.

Hannah laughed.

Twenty years, two husbands, three college educations, and many moves went by. The sisters were scattered across the country.

Hannah was busy with her second child. While she was home on maternity leave, she vowed to tackle her to-do list. One item reminded her to get the ruby and pearl ring cleaned and valued for insurance purposes. When Chet came home for lunch, Hannah grabbed the car keys from his hand and raced past him out the door. "Be back in a few minutes, and lunch is on the table," she said without breaking her stride.

On the way to the jeweler's store, Hannah allowed herself a fantasy. The jeweler would call over all the clerks in the store and the watchmaker in the back. "This is a priceless ruby," he would say. "Where did you get this?"

Hannah planned to be modest but forthright. "My grandfather was once very wealthy. This is just one piece of jewelry he gave my grandmother for her birthday."

Family

When she arrived the store was crowded. The jeweler took her ring and waited to view it under the scope. Hannah slowly inspected the display cases as he inspected the ring. He jotted a few notes on a piece of paper.

"Ma'am?" The white-haired man turned to Hannah.

"This is a wonderful example," he said slowly, "of a synthetic garnet put in a classical Victorian setting of composite metal."

Hannah gasped. "You mean it's not a real ruby?"

"No, ma'am," he said, "but it sure is pretty. You don't see many like this unless you are in the antique business. An antique dealer might be able to put a value on it, but as a piece of jewelry, it has no monetary value."

That night, after the phone rates went down, Hannah called her sisters.

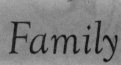

Family

BLESSING

Never let possessions come between me and the people
I love. Keep me from becoming too attached to things
that I perceive as giving me elevated status.
All that glitters is not gold.

1) We all have unconscious information we've absorbed from our
families. This information may or may not be correct. Journal
about the "truths" you accept about your family. You might
include "truths" about the skills of family members, "truths"
about the way the world works, and particularly "truths" about
who you are.

_____

_____

_____

_____

_____

_____

_____

_____

_____

_____

_____

_____

_____

_____

_____

Family

2) On a piece of paper, write a "truth" at the top. Divide the paper into two columns. In the left column, write down why you agree with the "truth." In the right column write down, reasons you think the "truth" might be wrong.

A TRUTH: _____

_____

_____

<u>AGREE</u>   <u>DISAGREE</u>

Family

3) If you have family members whose judgment you trust, you might wish to discuss a "truth" with that person. Do they have the same belief system? If they disagree with the "truth," why? How do they think that "truth" came to be accepted by the family?

_____

_____

_____

_____

_____

_____

_____

4) Make a list of new "truths" your family has not yet accepted. How do these new "truths" compare to the old "truths?"

❑ _____

❑ _____

❑ _____

❑ _____

❑ _____

❑ _____

❑ _____

❑ _____

❑ _____

❑ _____

❑ _____

❑ _____

Family

5) Create a script for debunking an old "truth" you've decided is inaccurate. You'll want to begin your comment with "I think" or "I feel" or "I believe." Don't attack or argue, but do assert that you challenge the accepted "truth." Be willing to offer a difference of opinion and then move on to another topic. Your job is not to convince others that you are right, but to put others on notice that you don't necessarily blindly accept their version of the "truth."

Work

Work
Day 12
Say Thank You

L acy Singer sat at her desk and looked out the window. The rain fell steadily, marking the sixth day in a row without sunshine. Disheartened, Lacy began to straighten her papers before making a real stab at getting work done. The phones in the real estate office were quiet and the day would not begin in earnest for another half hour.

The pile of magazines slid on the floor as Lacy tried to stuff them back on the bookshelf. Holding the magazines with one hand and balancing herself with the other, Lacy shoved them again. This time, one magazine popped out of the bunch and landed, open, at her feet.

The pages fell open to a picture of a woman in her seventies. She wore a gay hat and a scarf jauntily around her throat. Lacy recognized her as a sales superstar. Suddenly, Lacy felt herself transported back into time, to the beginning of her career. She could remember her husband Dan tossing a cassette tape through the air where it landed in Lacy's lap. "This came in a packet of sales materials we bought at the office. I sure don't have any use for it," he snorted. "Don't say I never gave you nothing."

The next day, Lacy played the tape while driving to work. The speaker told of her start in selling and of the hardships she had overcome. She explained the basics of selling, and the presenter encouraged women to get into this exciting field "where your income is only limited by your enthusiasm and desire."

Work

That afternoon, while making the men in the office their third pot of coffee, Lacy pulled the help wanted ads from the trash. Her secretarial job bored her, and her marriage was in trouble. But on her salary, she couldn't even think about leaving Dan. Yet, living with him had become more difficult by the day. In fact, when she had dropped off some papers for him at work last week his boss had asked her, "Has Dan told you that I suggested he go get help?" Lacy had only shaken her head "No," and kept on walking. She had been asking him to go with her to counseling for years. But what could she do?

She could sell. She would sell. The lady on the tape did it. So could she.

So began the journey that led her to this office. Now, with a new life, Lacy remembered the tape she had heard so long ago. And, she wondered, "Does this woman know how much she helped me?"

Inspired, Lacy sat down at the computer and whipped out an e-mail message. "Dear...You don't know me but you've had a tremendous influence on my life..." With the quick push of the send button, the e-mail message zipped across the miles, and Lacy returned to the pile of phone messages from prospects.

A week passed. The phone rang. "May I speak to Lacy Singer?" asked a warbly woman's voice. "This is she," clipped Lacy with a quick glance out the window where the parking lot glistened with rain.

"Thank you for your kind note." And with that the woman began to cry. "My husband has been so ill, and he was having an awful day, and your e-mail about my tapes meant so much. It helped me get through the day. Thank you. Thank you so much."

Work

BLESSING

*Today I am blessed by many who have touched
my life in ways they can't imagine.*

1) Make a list of people who have had a positive influence on
your life. The people can be living or dead. Consider putting this
list in a special place, like a file, where you can add to it.

☐ _____
☐ _____
☐ _____
☐ _____
☐ _____
☐ _____
☐ _____
☐ _____
☐ _____
☐ _____
☐ _____
☐ _____
☐ _____
☐ _____
☐ _____

2) Choose someone from the list who is dead. Write that person
a thank you note. Keep the thank you note in the file with your
people of positive influence.

Work

3) How did you feel after writing the thank you note? Journal about the experience.

_____

_____

_____

_____

_____

_____

_____

_____

4) Choose someone from the list who is living. Write that person a thank you note. Make a copy of the note for your file and mail a copy to the person.

5) How did you feel after writing the thank you note? Journal about the experience. Compare and contrast how you felt about writing a person who is dead and one who is living.

_____

_____

_____

_____

_____

_____

_____

_____

Work

Day 13
Where the Answer Is

"Rats." The press-on nail on her pinky was coming off again. Mallory rummaged through a drawer for the tube of super glue that had become her constant companion. Ringing up groceries all day long caused havoc with her nails. She'd grab a 5-lb. bag of potatoes and feel the nail twist off. Her grip would often slip on a six-pack and a nail would go flying. Once, a bemused man stood with his mouth open as a blood-red missile sailed past his head. "Well, I'll be," he muttered. She had to laugh.

So, hey, it was tough on her nails. Otherwise she loved her job. The money was good, and her insurance benefits were all paid. The hours were flexible, and she and Donnie could work around his schedule and the kids' school schedule, too.

But the temptation was awful. Everywhere she turned, she saw food. In the deli were those yummy sandwiches with chicken salad drenched in mayo, in the bakery she'd discovered fruit tarts, and the samplings on Saturdays were enough to drive her wild! In the six months she'd been working for Donaldson's Fine Foods, she'd put on 20 pounds. Not only by eating at work, but also by procrastinating on exercising and opening the refrigerator at home every chance she got.

Life had become more stressful when she went back to work. It wasn't Donnie's fault that his job on the highway crew had become so insecure. The old boss retired and the new department head didn't seem to value the seniority Donnie had so

Work

carefully earned. Then, too, who could have predicted little Brucie would need braces. Or that Bethany would beg for piano lessons. Or that their house would need a new washer, dryer and furnace all in the span of six months.

Her job helped her family, and she did enjoy meeting so many different people from all walks of life. Donaldson's had a very exclusive clientele, but Mallory quickly learned that when presented with a cheerful smile, each could become a friendly encounter.

"Hello," said a woman wheeling a cart into the check out lane. She was wearing that gorgeous black leather jacket Mallory had seen in the window of a local department store. Her pretty brunette bob covered her eyes as she reached into her basket and tossed a bag of Snickers bars onto the belt. Then followed two bags of Snowcaps, a bag of chocolate chip cookies, and a bag of peanut M n' Ms.

Mallory laughed. "Are you having a party?"

"No, I'm just feeling nervous."

That night after supper, Mallory pulled an index card from the back of her recipe box. She borrowed a colored marker from Bethany's art supplies. Neatly, she printed the same message three times: The Answer Isn't Here.

She took a piece of masking tape and taped a card to the refrigerator and to the outside of the pantry doors. Then she left the kids to work on their homework at the kitchen table and took her magazine into the living room, away from her temptations.

Work

BLESSING

Food is to fuel our bodies. We are blessed by the joys of its tastes and fragrances. Help me to realize, though, that food is not an answer to my problems.

1) Make a list of places you look for comfort.

❏ _____
❏ _____
❏ _____
❏ _____
❏ _____
❏ _____
❏ _____
❏ _____
❏ _____
❏ _____
❏ _____
❏ _____

2) Are all of those places healthy for you? Are there places you should be turning away from? What is and isn't working?

_____
_____
_____
_____
_____

Work

3) Practice eating mindfully. Put on soft music. Use good china. Add a slice of lemon to your water. Eat slowly, paying attention to each morsel. Journal about the experience.

_____

_____

_____

_____

_____

_____

_____

_____

4) Begin to purchase "one perfect" food. Instead of buying lots of food, buy "one perfect" apple or "one perfect" piece of candy. Journal about the experience of looking forward to and eating "one perfect" piece of food.

_____

_____

_____

_____

_____

_____

_____

_____

Work

5) Create cards that say "The Answer Isn't Here." Post them around your house.

The Answer Isn't Here

6) Write a list of positive and healthy ways to comfort yourself.

❑ _____

❑ _____

❑ _____

❑ _____

❑ _____

❑ _____

❑ _____

❑ _____

❑ _____

❑ _____

❑ _____

Work

Day 14
The Heavy Burden

"Then, he forgot the sign-up sheets, and we had to pay the hotel to run off more. At a quarter a page! Do you have any idea what that did to our overall costs? We're way over budget, and it's all his fault. I can't believe I'm going to have to work with John Albright again next year," Allison finally took a breath.

Anne couldn't blame her. Albright managed to single-handedly mess up every project he became involved in. Their nonprofit association was currently dealing with budget concerns, program snafus, and angry members. Anne herself had worked extra hours trying to pick up the pieces Albright had left in his wake.

"How that jerk ever got elected is beyond me," Allison was back to her tirade. She was furious. "I can't stand him, and I'm tired of dealing with him. But my boss assigned me to this association, and I can't quit now."

Anne was in the same situation. She, too, had many problems with Albright. As she listened to the other woman go on and on, she thought about her boss and why he had insisted she join this association. Then she realized, Albright had a big problem, bigger than he realized. If his mission was to improve his standing among his peers, he had blown it. If his goal—as was hers and others—was to eventually turn these contacts into business leads, he had lost his opportunity. Suddenly, she found herself feeling sorry for Albright. As much as she had suffered from his ineptitude, he had suffered more. What he didn't know, and

Work

wouldn't know for a long time to come, was exactly how many bridges he had burned.

"What should we do? I want to see him impeached!" said the other woman.

Anne cleared her throat and spoke slowly and softly, "Oh, no, Allison. Impeaching is too good for the rascal. There is only one punishment to fit a crime like this. I say we kill him!"

A stunned silence followed. Then both women laughed. By the time they hung up, they had discussed new options for dealing with Albright, and both felt much better.

Once I pulled an apple off a tree in a wooded area near my house. The apple knocked into a hornets' nest which was concealed in the leaves. The hornets attacked me. One managed to get inside my blouse and sting me over and over.

Holding a grudge is like having a hornet in your blouse. Most people are hurting themselves more than they are hurting you. Don't contribute your energy to theirs. Shake the hornet out of your clothes and move on.

Work

BLESSING

I can let go of my disappointments in others. Help me to see situations with new eyes. Help me to move on.

1) Make a list of "hornets" that sting you. How long have these angry thoughts been a part of your life?

❏ _____

_____

❏ _____

_____

❏ _____

_____

❏ _____

_____

❏ _____

_____

❏ _____

_____

❏ _____

_____

❏ _____

_____

2) Next to each "hornet," write a blessing. Thank the "hornet" for the lesson you learned. If you haven't learned a lesson, thank the "hornet" for the lesson you are in the process of learning.

Work

3) Write the name of each "hornet" on a piece of paper. Put the paper or papers in a fireproof bowl. Light the "hornet" and bless them. See the "hornets" as perfect just the way they are. Journal about the experience.

_____

_____

_____

_____

_____

_____

_____

_____

_____

_____

4) Forgive yourself. Write a note to yourself that it is time to move on.

_____

_____

_____

_____

_____

5) Make a note on your calendar to check your progress with giving up your "hornets." If you need to, revisit this exercise.

Work

Day 15
The Pond

"They didn't let me go. I quit."

Laurie reminded herself that she chose to leave the clothing store where she had worked for two years. But even as she repeated these words that had become a mantra to her, she felt the tears welling up in her eyes. Her throat tightened and hurt.

It's not fair! From deep inside her the words came like a scream.

She shook her head and finished getting dressed. Every day started the same, now that she was unemployed. No matter how good her intentions, she couldn't get herself out of bed in the morning. Her husband, Jim, didn't push her. He knew how much her job had meant to her.

"Take your time," he'd said. "Take a break. We can cut back on our expenses and you can regroup. Maybe you don't want to go back into retail. Give yourself a chance to see what you want before you job hunt again."

Job hunt? How could you job hunt when all you wanted to do was cry?

An hour passed. She had pulled on a pair of sweat pants and a sweat shirt. The March sun was trying to peek through the spring rain clouds. Maybe a walk would do her good.

Work

It was still early when she reached the pond. A mist of fog sat on the surface of the water as the morning temperature bumped into the night's chill. In the distance, she heard the honks of Canadian geese. Without thinking, Laurie began walking on the path around the pond. As she walked, she noticed bits of garbage, an empty package of cigarettes, a cola can, and a wrapper from a burger. She picked up the debris. By the time she came back to her starting point on the path, both hands were filled with junk. "Next time," she vowed, "I will bring a garbage bag."

So she did the next day. She filled it with cups, cans and soggy tennis balls that had been hit out of bounds from the nearby tennis courts and rolled into the pond. As she walked back with the black plastic bag, she felt a small but warming sense of accomplishment. Two houses before hers she spotted a tiny cluster of blue flowers poking their sleepy heads through the spring earth. Later that day, she lingered over a pot of crocuses at the grocery store. As she made her selection, she also decided to buy a sturdy bunch of asparagus to cook that night with dinner.

One day at a time, Laurie rebuilt her life. The walks around the pond became her central focus. Slowly, the walks seemed to lead to other pleasures, unexpected and unplanned. By midsummer, her life had developed a routine.

"What are your plans?" Wilma leaned over the cup of coffee and looked squarely at Laurie.

Laurie fiddled with a piece of quiche. "I don't know. I don't know if I ever want to work again."

Work

Wilma laughed. "Oh, Laurie, you will! You will. But you'll go back when you decide that you miss it, and not until then."

Wilma was right. At the end of June, Laurie was standing in a clothing store when the manager asked, "Didn't you once work for...?" Two hours later, Laurie was offered the position of assistant manager. The job was everything she could want, and the schedule left mornings free for a walk around the pond.

Work

BLESSING

By taking time to reconnect with the natural world I
can re-center my inner world. When I am
centered, life makes sense again.

1) Close your eyes and conjure up a scene in nature. Write a
description of the place you saw in your mind's eye.

_____

_____

_____

_____

_____

_____

_____

_____

_____

_____

2) Make a few notes about places near to your home or your
work where you could be part of nature. Plan a visit.

_____

_____

_____

_____

_____

_____

Work

3) Journal about the local places. Make notes on what you see.

_____
_____
_____
_____
_____
_____
_____
_____
_____
_____

4) As you go about your daily routine, look for nature everywhere. Whether it's a leaf stuck to your windshield or a ladybug that's crawled into a crevice in your office, nature comes to us. Journal about the nature you see.

_____
_____
_____
_____
_____
_____
_____
_____

5) If you can't see nature regularly, create a notebook of natural scenes. Journal beneath the pictures you choose.

Work

Day 16
Victim No More

The quiet rustle of papers dominated the room as the two departments studied the marketing figures. Once or twice, a scratching pen making notes broke the silence. Then, one by one, people closed the report and looked back at the man sitting at the head of the table.

Ballistic Bob, they called him. He was known as a brilliant marketer, but a bad boy with a temper that matched the destructive capabilities of a nuclear warhead.

Belinda had worked for him for three months now. Although she'd heard of his famous fury, she had never seen him in action. After all, she had given him no reason. Belinda was a meticulous worker who checked and rechecked every project for accuracy. A list-maker, she took copious notes and highlighted them at the end of each day to make sure she had followed up on each request that came her way.

She sat back and watched the group with satisfaction. She had used an old marketing report as a template and prepared this one with the new, updated figures. Twice she had run copies past Bob for approval. Now, seeing the reaction of the team, she was pleased.

"I don't see the projected figures," said Sam Ungerman. "Where are they?"

Work

Belinda's stomach did a flip. No one had told her that the reports always included a projection. The original hadn't had one. Bob hadn't mentioned it.

"Where's the projection, Belinda?" Bob turned to her with icy blue eyes. "You did put one together, didn't you?"

"No, sir," she managed to speak softly but clearly. "I wasn't aware that projections were a normal part of the report."

"What? How can we work without the darn projections? Do you mean to tell me you've wasted all our time by leaving out the most important part of the report? How could you be so stupid? What the heck were you thinking? What do you expect me to tell Cromwell when he asks?" and with that opening salvo, Ballistic Bob dissolved into a flurry of curse words, all directed toward Belinda.

She didn't remember who adjourned the meeting. Nor could she recall how she stumbled into the ladies' restroom. Belinda only knew she had to run and hide before everyone in the company could see the tears streaming down her face.

"What are you going to do?" asked her friend Marla during their break. "You can't fight back. He checked your work and over-looked the projections. He knows it. So do all the people who were in the meeting."

Belinda shuddered. She couldn't quit. She and Brad had bought their first house three weeks ago. The house payments took both their salaries with no money to spare. Finding a new job would take weeks, even months.

Work

"I'm going to face him," she decided. "Help me figure out what to say."

At the end of the day, Belinda knocked on the door of Bob's office. "May I speak with you for two minutes?" she asked.

He grunted and waved her over to the chair positioned directly across from his huge, walnut desk. Then, Bob wove his fingers together behind his head and rocked back in his cushy burgundy leather chair. "What's up?"

"When you talk to me the way you did in the meeting this morning, we both look unprofessional," she began clearly. Her voice was neither loud nor soft, and she held her hands together in her lap to keep them from trembling. "The next time there is a problem, all you need to do is point it out to me. We don't need to look bad in front of the other people in this company. What happened this morning doesn't need to happen again. I can be far more productive if you quietly tell me what I missed than if you raise your voice."

Bob's face never changed. If he heard her, he never gave her any indication. Then he mumbled, "Okay."

Bob never again took her to task in front of their co-workers. Nor did he ever mention Belinda's comments. Six months later Belinda posted for—and was promoted to—a job in another department.

Work

BLESSING

I don't have to act like a victim when confronted by people who are unkind to me. Please help me to stand up for myself. It is my job to indicate to others how I wish to be treated.

1) *Think about a situation where you feel like a victim. Make some notes on the situation.*

_____

_____

_____

_____

_____

_____

_____

_____

_____

_____

_____

_____

_____

_____

_____

Work

2) Ask yourself if you could be misinterpreting the situation. Write down at least two explanations for the situation that do NOT include you being a victim.

EXPLANATION 1: _____

_____

_____

_____

_____

EXPLANATION 2: _____

_____

_____

_____

_____

3) If you still believe you are being victimized by the situation, write down how you'd like to see the situation change. Structure your sentences so that they begin with "I want..." or "I need..." or "I feel..."

_____

_____

_____

_____

_____

_____

_____

_____

Work

4) *Think about the other person involved in the situation. How might they benefit by changing the situation so that you aren't a victim? Remember: People who victimize other people do not feel good about themselves. How could a change help the other person feel better?*

_____

_____

_____

_____

_____

_____

_____

_____

_____

_____

5) *Write a sample script in which you request a change in your relationship. Base your suggestion on how it might benefit the other person as well as you.*

_____

_____

_____

_____

_____

_____

_____

_____

Parenting

Parenting

Day 17
A Coloring Fool

"**M**ama, do! Mama, do!"

Lynn felt the left edge of her sweater being pulled. She looked down from the recipe card she was reading. Marcie stood at her side tugging with impatience.

"Mama, do!"

"Oh, babe," sighed Lynn. All day long Marcie pulled and asked, repeating her requests like a mynah bird. The constant chirping accompanied Lynn all through the house. As much as she loved her tiny daughter, occasionally she found herself fighting a scream. The never-ending demands interrupted every train of thought, leaving Lynn at the end of the day with a dozen unfinished projects.

"Colo?" Marcie waved a handful of crayons.

"Hey, you aren't supposed to have those," said Lynn, scooping up the toddler.

A few minutes later, they both sat at the kitchen table coloring. Marcie jabbed at her paper with fat crayons and markers. Lynn began to color in a large eggplant, moving the deep purple crayon slowly back and forth across the wide expanse of paper. Fifteen, twenty minutes went by. Lynn lost all track of the time. Marcie was still absorbed.

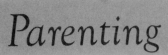

Parenting

Lynn studied her eggplant. The smooth colors seemed so right. The background of light cornflower blue set off the deep, dark black-purple. The lush green leaves offered a bright contrast. She hung her picture and Marcie's on the refrigerator door. "At least," she murmured, "I finished something today."

The next day, Lynn found herself eager to sit down and color again. She wondered if the magic would work two days in a row. At the end of their coloring session, she noticed Marcie was calmer and she felt more relaxed, too.

Now Lynn grabs her crayons whenever she feels stressed. She's collected an entire set of adult coloring books with themes as diverse as orange crate labels, Greek mythological figures, and birds of North America. She and Marcie think of their coloring time together as that time in the afternoon when they both wind down. And, their refrigerator has never been more festive.

Parenting

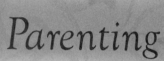

BLESSING

When I am feeling stressed, help me to find a task I can do. Guide me to choose an activity that will soothe me and give me a sense of accomplishment.

1) Make a list of creative activities you once enjoyed as a child. Or make a list of activities you always wanted to try but haven't.

❏ _____
❏ _____
❏ _____
❏ _____
❏ _____
❏ _____
❏ _____
❏ _____
❏ _____
❏ _____
❏ _____
❏ _____
❏ _____
❏ _____
❏ _____
❏ _____

2) Look at that list and circle one thing that most appeals to you.

Parenting

3) Consider what might be a first step toward that activity. Do you need equipment? Should you find a book on the subject? Could you visit a place that sells related merchandise? Choose a first step and write it down.

_____

_____

_____

4) Explore your first step. Journal about how it went.

_____

_____

_____

_____

_____

_____

_____

_____

5) Journal about the reasons you don't allow yourself to enjoy more creative activities. Be honest about what holds you back. Don't use time as the excuse. Tackle your restraints by noting what you could do to move forward.

_____

_____

_____

_____

_____

_____

Parenting

Day 18
The Errand Runner

Buzz, buzz, buzz. The phone on Judy's desk throbbed. She tried to ignore the sound. Two more seconds, just two, and she'd have this column of numbers added up and...

"Yes?"

"It's time for my break. Get me a Diet Coke, would you? Oh, and some of those pretzels that I like. By the way, have you finished copying those surveys? I told you I needed them by noon."

Judy glanced at her desk. In her to-do pile, somewhere, were the surveys. She'd come in extra-early this morning to get them done. Now... did she have correct change for the vending machine?

"Okay, Mom, I'll be there in a jiffy."

Carmen stuck her head around the partition that separated the two workers. "I thought you told me you were having a talk with your mama," said the older woman. "Didn't you? Girlfriend, you are nuts. I wouldn't let anyone treat me like that. That's nonsense." Carmen tapped a long burgundy nail on Judy's desk. And I don't care if she is your mama, you're crazy!"

Judy pulled the surveys out of the pile and rummaged through her desk drawer for change. "Got change for a buck?" she asked, avoiding Carmen's dark look of disgust.

Parenting

That weekend at her grandmother's, Judy tried not to think about work. She loaded up a big stalk of celery with pimento cheese spread and crunched loudly as she chewed.

"How's work, lambie?" MeMaw studied her oldest grandchild as she ate. "Do you like working in the same department as your mother?"

Judy stopped chewing. She hesitated. Then she spilled her guts. "MeMaw, I don't know what to do! Mom calls me three times a day to get her a Coke or a snack. She asks me to do part of her work. I'm coming in early to get her stuff done and mine! All my co-workers think I'm crazy, and I hate it. I know I should be appreciative. She did get me the job, after all. But, I didn't expect her to treat me like this. I don't work for her!"

"OOOOwwwee." MeMaw shook her white head of hair and laughed. "My little bunny is up to her old tricks. Didn't you ever talk to your Auntie Alice?"

"'Bout what?"

"About your mama," said MeMaw as her sides shook in laughter. "Your mama takes the cake when it comes to being lazy. She was always getting her little sister Alice to do her homework and her chores. Then one day Alice got smart. Stood up to your mama is what she did. She said, "Don't be pulling that stuff on me any more. Your mama got the religion. Though it looks like she's needing a refresher course for sure!"

On Monday Judy's phone rang.

"Get me a Diet Coke and some cheese and peanut butter crackers."

Parenting

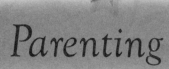

Judy took a deep breath. "Sorry, Mama, you must have the wrong number," and she hung up.

From around the cubicle came Carmen's gorgeous mop of jet black curls. "Well, it's about time. Looks like today's Independence Day. Good for you!"

And the two women laughed.

Parenting

BLESSING

It can be difficult to tell some people, "No." I can take control and decide what is appropriately my responsibility and what is not.

1) Write about taking control of a situation in your life that is an unnecessary burden.

_____

_____

_____

_____

_____

_____

_____

_____

_____

_____

2) Brainstorm and write what you wished you had said to the family member.

_____

_____

_____

_____

_____

Parenting

3) Review your "pretend" script. Is there a way to refuse the request without sounding harsh?

_____

_____

_____

_____

_____

_____

_____

_____

4) Decide on a strategy for coping with a family member's problematic behavior. Brainstorm a variety of solutions.

_____

_____

_____

_____

_____

_____

_____

_____

_____

_____

Parenting

5) Ask yourself what would happen if you simply said, "That doesn't work for me."

_____
_____
_____
_____
_____
_____
_____
_____
_____

6) Write what you fear might happen if you refuse a family member's request. How likely is that to happen?

_____
_____
_____
_____
_____
_____
_____
_____
_____
_____
_____

Parenting

Day 19
Saying "Yes" to Life

Virginia grabbed Rory's cup as he began to transfer water from it into his soup bowl.

"No," she said calmly and firmly. She turned back to her pork chop for another bite.

Out of the corner of her eye she saw Rory slip a piece of meat under the table. The tip of the dog's nose poked around beneath the boy's hand.

"No," she repeated. "We don't feed the dog at the table. Now we have to wash your hands."

The three-year-old slid down from his chair and followed her obediently into the bathroom. Virginia turned on the tap, soaped his hands and turned her back to grab a towel. By the time she had turned around, Rory had squirted hand lotion on the mirror.

"No, lotion is for hands not for mirrors," said Virginia, trying her best to mimic his preschool teachers. With a corner of the towel, she mopped up the lotion. Then she wet toilet paper and tried to return the mirror to its initial luster. When they walked back into the kitchen, she noticed that Doug, her husband, had finished his food and was ready to go downstairs to watch the Bulls play an exhibition game. Increasingly, she felt a sense of frustration at mealtimes. While she struggled with Rory, Doug blocked out the entire domestic drama and ate a leisurely meal. By the time Rory and he had finished, her food was cold. Often she wound up

Parenting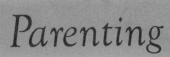

grabbing bites from her plate and theirs on the way to the dishwasher. If she turned her back on Rory for a moment, she turned back to find a mess that would take at least fifteen minutes to clean. The child wasn't naughty, but he was insatiably curious.

"Doug, could you sit with us a while longer?"

"Sure." He sat quietly as Rory finished picking at his plate and as Virginia raced through her meal.

"Popsecupa?" asked Rory hopefully.

Virginia groaned. Feeding him a Popsicle was an invitation to a mess. He dripped them all over the kitchen, losing chunks as he bit from one side, and leaving sticks for the dog to find and chew on. He had, however, cleaned his plate.

She stalled. Leaning her head in her hands, she turned her face away from the child and looked out the doors to their deck. Then pudgy hands reached up and captured her face to pull it nose to nose with his. "Popsecupa?" he repeated patiently.

With a hug, she answered.

"I'd like one, too, babe," said Doug. "What flavors do we have?"

The two bent their heads over the assortment of red, purple, blue and yellow confections. Doug chose red, Virginia picked a yellow for herself and began to unwrap Rory's favorite purple. As she peeled the paper from the iced treat, she had an idea.

"Let's go outside to eat."

The family reassembled on the deck. Rory happily dripped his "Popsecupa" while he sucked until his lips turned purple. Doug stood leaning against the deck railing. As Virginia squinted up to

Parenting

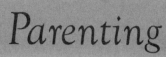

talk with him, a flash of color caught her attention. She rose and walked to the railing. Floating in the distance, beyond the emerald green soybean field that stretched out behind their yard, was a blue hot air balloon.

"Look! Look!" she shouted.

They all turned in time to see the first balloon followed by a tiny black spot. The spot grew to be another balloon, which was orange- and blue-striped. A few heartbeats later, the two were joined by a yellow and orange balloon with lettering, a navy balloon with a corporate logo, a crimson balloon in the shape of a tomato, and a gold balloon with a black beer label.

The family slurped their Popsicles and watched eagerly. The spectacle lasted for nearly half an hour. Rory pointed out his favorites to Doug and Virginia. In between balloon sitings, the couple had the chance to talk a little about their day. By the time they returned to the house, a tired but happy Rory was covered in purple goo and ready for a bath and bed.

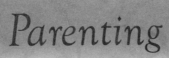

Parenting

BLESSING

Let me say, "Yes," more often when life beckons me.
Life is about being messy and curious. If I stress out by
trying to make life neat and clean, I will miss chances
to enjoy what life has to offer. Teach me to say, "Yes."

1) Journal about the reasons you like life to be neat and
controlled.

_____

_____

_____

_____

_____

_____

_____

_____

_____

2) Do you harbor any fears that are outmoded?

_____

_____

_____

_____

_____

_____

_____

Parenting

3) Journal about times you said "No" to life. What do you think you missed by saying "No"?

_____

_____

_____

_____

_____

_____

_____

_____

_____

_____

_____

4) Write a statement of intent to stop and smell the roses. Make a pledge to pause to wonder.

_____

_____

_____

_____

_____

_____

_____

_____

_____

Parenting

5) Recall a time in the past when you stopped to enjoy what life offered. How did it make you feel?

_____

_____

_____

_____

_____

_____

_____

_____

_____

_____

_____

_____

6) If you take the time to enjoy life as a result of your journaling work, write down how you felt.

_____

_____

_____

_____

_____

_____

_____

_____

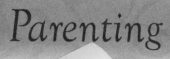

Parenting

Day 20
United States of Motherhood

T he luminous numbers clicked as the time moved from 1:59 a.m. to 2:00 a.m. I shifted the weight on my lap and moved my newborn son from one breast to the other.

Quickly, Michael made it clear that he was no longer interested in nursing. I shifted him to my shoulder and patted his warm little back, waiting for that satisfying burp that would signal his stomach's acceptance of my late night offerings. Beneath me, I felt my legs growing numb and tingly. Even with a cushion, this wooden rocker was painful to sit in for long periods, night after night.

From the light of the street lamp, I could see shadows in my son's room. The quiet of the evening settled around us, but still Michael wouldn't sleep.

"Colic," said the pediatrician. "We don't know why it happens. He'll grow out of it at about three months. We suspect their digestive system starts to mature by then. You're home free the day he passes gas. Sorry."

Sorry! Sorry? My patience and my body were worn thin. All the baby books had profiled an infant who would spend most of his early first year snoozing. With my Southern hemisphere sporting more stitches than a Quaker's sampler, and my hair coming out in chunks, I was a poster child for postpartum distress. My sanity began to unravel as I hallucinated that I was part of an ancient Mayan culture where babies were the ultimate, often deady rites

Parenting

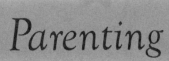

of entering womanhood. The next day I dragged myself, baby and car seat, into the doctor's office. I had been up forty-eight hours straight. Michael had slept a mere forty-five minutes during that two-day eternity. Thirty of those forty-five minutes had been on the car ride to the clinic. If I could only stay awake long enough, I might be able to drive to Alaska and back in three months.

Thank goodness, the drugs the doctor prescribed to ease Michael's system began to take effect. His naps did fall into a general pattern, still far, far shorter than listed by the experts. But nighttime was party-time for Mr. Mike. I read books about letting him scream. I listened to tapes by experts on walking away. I tried gizmos and gadgets that shook me and his bed like a blender set on high. But, I couldn't walk away or relegate him to machinery. He was obviously in distress. The least I could do, I reasoned, was sit with him through the long and painful nights while he squirmed and struggled to fall asleep.

So, we rocked. We rocked the circumference of the earth. Then we rocked our way to the moon. Tonight we had been rocking toward Pluto. I brushed the velvety crown of his head. So dear, so soft like chick down. I curled and uncurled his tiny fingers. I struggled with my anger. I sat here alone with him as my husband slept. Why wasn't he sleeping? How long could I go without rest? A wave of shame broke over me. Wasn't I blessed to have him? Wouldn't a million women give anything to be holding a child?

Then as I glimpsed the moon moving behind a cloud, a thought came to me. A million women. A million mothers. A million babies.

Parenting

Suddenly, I realized that I was not alone. All over the globe, women were holding their babies. Some were lucky enough to sit in rockers. Some crouched on the ground. Some had a roof over their heads, as I did. Many more were exposed to the elements, shielding their babies from the rain, the snow and the sun.

We were all alike. We held our children and prayed. Some would not live to see their children grown. Some children would not live out the year. Some would die of hunger. Some from bullets or sickness.

But for a moment, under the same pale moon, we were all together. Rocking our babies and praying. Loving them and hoping.

From that night on, I viewed my time with Michael differently. The fatigue never went away. The seat never seemed any softer. But as I sat with him I felt the company of a million, billion, trillion mothers holding our babies in our arms.

Parenting

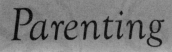

BLESSING

I am part of worldwide family. We share the same hopes and dreams. I am blessed to live in this country, to enjoy this standard of living, and to dream these dreams.

1) For this exercise, take your journal to a place where you can watch people. Choose one or two people to think about. Try to imagine what their parents hoped for them.

_____

_____

_____

_____

_____

_____

_____

_____

2) Read about a person in another country. Try to imagine your-self in that person's situation.

_____

_____

_____

_____

_____

_____

Parenting

3) Light a candle and pray for peace. Write your prayer and say it out loud.

_____

_____

_____

_____

_____

_____

_____

_____

_____

_____

4) Go outside under the stars. Realize that these are the same stars that lit up the sky for Shakespeare, Einstein and Mother Teresa. Know that you are part of the same universe of humanity that has lived before us. Write about feeling connected.

_____

_____

_____

_____

_____

_____

_____

_____

_____

_____

_____

Parenting

_____

_____

_____

_____

_____

5) Smile at a child when no one else is looking. Write about the child's reaction and how you felt.

_____

_____

_____

_____

_____

_____

_____

_____

_____

_____

_____

_____

_____

Parenting

Day 21
Where Do Rainbows Go?

Storms in South Carolina are a lot like the tantrums of toddlers: They gather slowly, blow up with a lot of sound and fury, and quickly fade into nothingness.

After such a storm, my nephew Joshua and I walked the beach at Isle of Palms together. A small ghost crab raced over his foot, and he yelped in terror.

I laughed. "He won't hurt you. You're a giant to him. See him run?"

The beaches of South Carolina have always been my favorite place in the world, and I loved sharing with this four-year-old the wonders of the sea shore. I told him the stories my grandmother told me about the Angels and Devils fighting on the beach for the fate of the world. Then we found the transparent gold and black shells called "Angel's toenails" and "Devil's toenails" respectively.

"Oh, Josh, look!" Above our heads a double rainbow arched in magnificent colors and touched the horizon.

He shaded his eyes with his hand. "Aunt Jonie," he asked, "Where do the rainbows go?"

I thought about his question. "Actually, Josh, they don't go anywhere. They are always there. Just sometimes we can't see them."

Parenting

The next day, Joshua was killed when an unsecured gravestone in the cemetery of the French Huguenot Church in Charleston, S.C., crushed him to death. As we helped escort the stretcher bearing him out of the graveyard, we carried him over the graves of our ancestors. A part of me kept thinking, "This is so macabre that it must be a dream. Wake up! Wake up! Let it all be over."

But it wasn't. A few days later my sister and her husband filled a coffin with toys and the body of their son.

The next months were a haze of pain. I went to court and heard the judge pronounce the end of my marriage. I stumbled outside the dark corridors of the courthouse into the sun, and wondered if I was doomed to live my life alone forever.

Back at work, I did my job, but often I was in great emotional turmoil. The day I called on a toy store, a client of mine, I was overcome with sobs. As far as the eye could see was shelf after shelf of toys my nephew would never play with.

I really hit bottom the day I drove around a stopped school bus and nearly missed hitting a child. In the deep fog of my misery, life had become a blur. I had almost hurt another child while grieving for Josh!

I shook all the way back to my little apartment. Inside, I threw myself down on the narrow single bed and cried for hours. Finally, I slipped to my knees on the floor and prayed. "Help me, God. Help me. What kind of God are you to let a little boy die? How can I believe?" Then, slowly the words of the Lord's Prayer came back to me: "Give us this day…"

Parenting

The days we have on this earth are a gift. I could no more be angry at God for taking back his own than I could be angry at the library because my books were due. We are all on loan! The joy is that I knew Josh. And that joy was mine to keep forever.

"Give us this day." Josh's days were done. But, God had given me more days on this earth. What I did with them was up to me. I got up off my knees and began to feel alive for the first time in many months.

A few weeks later, I was driving when I happened to look up and see a rainbow. I pulled the car over to the side of the road and got out.

"Where do the rainbows go, Aunt Jonie?" The voice came to me.

And so did the answer: "They are always there. Just sometimes we can't see them." Those we love never leave us, but sometimes we can't see them.

Parenting

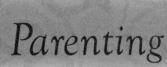

BLESSING

*Our lives are more precious when we recognize how
little time we truly have here on earth. Each of us
is a gift from God, and each day is also a gift
we must cherish. Let us never take each other
or our time here on earth for granted.*

*1) Make a list of those you love who can never leave you because
of this love. Note how they've influenced who you are.*

❑ _____

_____

❑ _____

_____

❑ _____

_____

❑ _____

_____

❑ _____

_____

❑ _____

_____

❑ _____

_____

❑ _____

_____

❑ _____

_____

Parenting

2) Light a candle and pray for those who have passed away. Choose one person to reminisce about and write down your memories.

_____

_____

_____

_____

_____

_____

_____

_____

_____

3) What can't you see that you know exists? Make a list. It might surprise you. (Hint: Be sure to include body parts and emotions. Although you've probably never seen your own heart, you surely know it exists.)

❑ _____

❑ _____

❑ _____

❑ _____

❑ _____

❑ _____

❑ _____

❑ _____

❑ _____

Parenting

4) Find a way to celebrate the life of someone who has passed on. Make a donation or do a good deed in that person's memory.

5) Create an honor roll of people you've never met whose lives have had an impact on yours. Although you may never meet these people, you can still appreciate their contribution to your life.

❏ _____

❏ _____

❏ _____

❏ _____

❏ _____

❏ _____

❏ _____

❏ _____

❏ _____

❏ _____

❏ _____

❏ _____

❏ _____

❏ _____

Friendship

Friendship

Day 22
All That I Have Left

"I'll be in town the twentieth," Linda told her friend Veronica. "I'm flying in for business. Can we get together?"

Veronica rustled a calendar in the background. "That's a Friday night, and I always have the entire family over for dinner. Please come. It will be a delight to see you."

After they said goodbye, Veronica hung up the phone and walked to the window. The shady residential street was quiet this early in the morning. The leaves of the maples cast shadows on the sidewalk. Imagine, she thought, me living in a house with a sidewalk not twenty feet from my front door. She, the woman who loved open spaces, had come to this. Then she jumped. House! House? No, this is an apartment. I don't even live in a house anymore.

Her hand brushed the photo frame on the coffee table. Milton, she thought, how could you have left me to figure out this mess?

What a shock she had had nine months ago when Milton died. Meticulous Milton, they all called him. Well, they were wrong. Milton had not left a will. The papers on the business were in total disarray. For months, Veronica had struggled to figure out what they owed and to whom. In the end, the attorneys walked away with more money than she had. The family beach house had to be sold. The big old cedar house with the broad porch in

Friendship

the front where she had raised her kids and collected her antiques had to be sold as well.

She had given away one possession after another so that she could squeeze into this tiny apartment with a view of a sidewalk. No longer would she sleep to the sound of spring peepers. Instead, her nights were filled with honking horns and slamming doors.

"Was that the door?" Veronica kept asking. A wisp of her hair fell over her face as she cut up cheese pizza into kid-size slices. To her left was one daughter, tossing fruit salad. To her right was a daughter-in-law slicing tomatoes into the green salad. Behind her was a grandchild playing with a stuffed blue bunny on the floor.

"Veronica!" The tiny guest threw her arms around the woman's neck. Veronica blinked back tears as she hugged Linda in return.

"Time for the blessing!" Her son-in-law passed around a basket filled with yarmulkes. Hands reached into the basket and covered heads popped up like spring mushrooms after a rain. Curt began to recite prayers in Hebrew, his voice rich and throaty. "Now for the Birchat Habanim, the Blessing of the Children!" A new prayer was chanted and hands touched the heads of all the children in the family. Then the entire group descended on the dining room table and hands grabbed for paper plates, pizza, fruit salad, green salad and paper cups filled with bubbling soft drinks.

"Let's go outside on the balcony and talk," Veronica took Linda by the arm. Once outside, she updated Linda on the financial

Friendship

morass and resulting nightmare. "When I visit my daughters and my sons and I see all my beautiful things. I gave each of them up, one by one. It's not over yet. There are still bills coming in. I've found a job. It doesn't pay much, but... What will I do? Linda, I've lost everything! My husband, my home, my things! I must be the unluckiest woman in the world!"

Linda looked at her friend. Then she looked inside the tiny apartment for a long time. "Veronica," she whispered, "look there," and she guided the woman's eyes to the mass of grandchildren, sons and daughters eating and talking and laughing inside the tiny apartment. "Veronica," repeated Linda, "you haven't lost everything. In fact, I think you are the wealthiest woman I know."

Friendship

BLESSING

*I am wealthy in proportion to the number of people
I have in my life. Please help me realize I am
not wealthy because of the things I own.*

1) Families are more than the people who are related to you
through marriage or blood. They are also the friends you invite to
be a permanent part of your life. List people whom you consider
to be your family.

❏ _____
❏ _____
❏ _____
❏ _____
❏ _____
❏ _____
❏ _____
❏ _____
❏ _____
❏ _____
❏ _____
❏ _____
❏ _____
❏ _____
❏ _____
❏ _____

Friendship

2) List family members who are your relatives.

- ❑ _____
- ❑ _____
- ❑ _____
- ❑ _____
- ❑ _____
- ❑ _____
- ❑ _____
- ❑ _____
- ❑ _____
- ❑ _____

3) Part of our wealth is our talents and abilities. What we know and what we have experienced can never be taken from us. Make an inventory of this wealth.

_____

_____

_____

_____

_____

_____

_____

_____

_____

_____

_____

_____

Friendship

4) Cut a green piece of paper the size of a dollar bill. On it list your true wealth, using the prior steps to help you.

_____

_____

_____

_____

_____

5) Keep your green paper in your wallet. Journal how you feel when you reach for money and find the green paper.

_____

_____

_____

_____

_____

_____

_____

_____

_____

_____

_____

_____

_____

_____

Friendship

Day 23
Arlene's Carrot Cake

Ommf. Leslie pushed the bulky stroller over the cobblestone parking lot. Sissy sat in the seat like a tubby princess, her eyes scrunched up against the warm September sun. Her rosebud lips pursed with concentration as she took in her surroundings—the row of tiny shops in front of them.

Leslie pushed again to dislodge the stuck wheel. She hoped the Cuisinart box that she had balanced in the back of the stroller wouldn't fall out as she gave the stroller yet another shove.

Inside The Seasoned Chef, Leslie felt a blast of cold air from the air-conditioner. The clerk's stare was almost as chilly. "May we help you?"

"Mrs. Rosen, please," asked Leslie, trying to ignore a trickle of sweat that was dangling from her left eyebrow. The clerk's eyes narrowed in disapproval but she picked up the phone and announced to the mythical Mrs. Rosen that "someONE is HERE to SEE you."

A well-rounded woman scurried from behind shelves and displays. "Let's see it," she quivered as Leslie lifted the Cuisinart box onto the counter.

"I can't get this to turn on this," explained Leslie as the older woman took the pieces from her hands.

Friendship

"You're trying to get this on backwards," said Mrs. Rosen as she deftly rotated the pieces and locked them together with a click. The two women practiced the move several times until Leslie began to load the pieces back into the box.

"Could I ask one other question? I mean, you've been so kind to help and all... Is it okay to cook with Crisco that's two years old? What's the expiration date on stuff like that?"

Mrs. Rosen's withered lips opened in a gasp. "I should say not. The freshest ingredients are the best." She drew herself up to her full height of 4' 11" and peered over the top of her half-glasses. "May I be so bold as to ask why this sudden interest in cooking?"

Leslie looked away in embarrassment. Then she looked at the top of Sissy's head, covered with ringlets. Finally she turned her frank glaze at Mrs. Rosen. "I have this recipe from my mother-in-law, who has passed away. It's my husband's favorite carrot cake. He and I are having....well, I thought making the cake would be a nice way to let him know I really am on his side. I tried to chop up the carrots in the blender, but... Then I remembered this machine. I never could figure it out. That's why I called."

Mrs. Rosen's face softened like a stick of butter left all night on the kitchen counter. "Do you have the recipe with you?"

The two heads, one blonde with curls and the other a short cap of grey, bent over the handwritten note card. Mrs. Rosen talked Leslie through the steps listed. They discussed ingredients, technique and cooking time. Before Leslie left the shop, she turned and spontaneously threw her arms around Mrs. Rosen and whispered, "Thanks."

Friendship

Sheldon finished his roast beef without a word and pushed his plate away.

"I made something special today," began Leslie. She uncovered the platter and sliced into the moist, fragrant carrot cake. With trembling hands, she put the plate in front of Sheldon.

"Mom's cake?" he asked. Then he took a bite. Over his face swept a cacophony of emotions. He looked at Leslie and smiled. "Thank you, honey," he said. "Thank you."

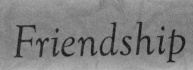

Friendship

BLESSING

Today I will dissolve the friction in my life as I make a special effort for someone I love. We talk so much about love when we could, instead, choose to illustrate our devotion. Today I will look for a way to show my love.

ARLENE'S CARROT CAKE

PART 1

1 1/2 cups Crisco or Spry

1 cup brown sugar, packed

2 cups grated carrots (if you use the food processor, consider adding extra cooking time because this adds moisture to the cake)

4 teaspoons lemon juice

2 whole eggs

PART 2

2 1/2 cups flour (sifted is okay, but heap in measuring cups)

1 1/2 teaspoons cinnamon

3/4 teaspoons nutmeg

1 teaspoon baking soda

1 teaspoon salt

2 teaspoons baking powder

Lightly mix all the ingredients from Part 2 together. Into a large bowl, stir together all the ingredients from Part 1. Add the ingredients from Part 2. Stir well. Put the mixture into a large ring mold. Even out the batter, but do not press down hard. Bake at 350 degrees for 35 minutes. This freezes well.

Friendship

1) Pay attention to people's hearts' desires. Make notes in your journal about the small comments people make that give you insight into what they value, need and want.

_____

_____

_____

_____

_____

_____

_____

_____

_____

2) Occasionally a person will show an interest in something that is well within their financial means, but they hold back on giving themselves permission to make a purchase or commitment. Have you seen this happen? Do you do this to yourself? Respond to this idea in your journaling.

_____

_____

_____

_____

_____

_____

_____

Friendship

3) *Give someone one of their hearts' desires. Journal about his or her response and the feeling you had.*

_____

_____

_____

_____

_____

_____

_____

_____

_____

_____

_____

4) *Make a list of actions or items you'd like to have in your life.*

_____

_____

_____

_____

_____

_____

_____

_____

_____

_____

Friendship

5) Can you give yourself one of your heart's desires? Why or why not?

_____

_____

_____

_____

_____

_____

_____

_____

_____

6) Cook a food that you enjoy and that comforts you. Share it with a friend. Journal about the experience.

_____

_____

_____

_____

_____

_____

_____

_____

_____

_____

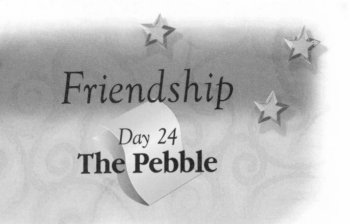

Friendship

Day 24
The Pebble

" Flight 726 to Omaha will be departing from Gate 6. We will be boarding the aircraft in fifteen minutes. Please have your boarding passes ready."

Kathie gathered her satchel and struggled with her coat. The carnation corsage pinned to the front of her suit made putting on the trench coat difficult. In fact, the coat would crush the flower. Kathie stopped and thought. Across the hallway a sour faced woman stacked magazines in a rack. She was ripping the plastic covers off bundles of print material in an angry way.

Kathie walked over to the woman.

"What do you want?" asked the woman, glaring at Kathie from under her armpit.

Kathie smiled and said softly, "I want to give you this." She held out the corsage to the woman. "Please take it."

The other woman rocked back on her heels. Her face relaxed as her hand reached for the red blossom. "Thanks."

Kathie boarded the plane. An older woman struggled to get her suitcase in the overhead bin. Two men sat nearby and watched. One ducked his head down into his newspaper to avoid the situation. The other turned to look out the window. The flight attendant stood at the end of the aisle and chatted

Friendship

with another attendant. The older woman tried to pick up her bag but had trouble lifting it above her waist.

"May I help?" Kathie kicked off her pumps and stepped onto the empty aisle seat. Then she hoisted the floral case above her head and into the bin.

"Thank you so much," said the white-haired woman. "I was worried about what I'd do."

The plane ride was uneventful. When the plane landed, one of the men who had watched Kathie struggle with the older woman's luggage lifted the floral bag easily from the overhead bin. He turned to the woman and presented it to her.

The flight attendant held the older woman's arm as she climbed slowly down the stairs onto the tarmac. The second attendant motioned to an airline employee who then grabbed the floral bag and carried it into the terminal.

Maybe we all need role models, thought Kathie, and maybe we are all role models for each other.

Friendship

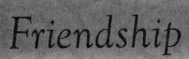

BLESSING

Guide me, whisper to me, and keep me vigilant. Don't let me overlook the chance to make life a little more pleasant for someone else. I know my good deeds find their way back to me.

1) Initiate a simple act of kindness toward a stranger. Give a compliment out loud rather than thinking it silently. Journal about the experience.

_____

_____

_____

_____

_____

_____

_____

2) Like the ripples radiating endlessly from a rock dropped in a pond, have you noticed acts of kindness that have a ripple effect? In the same way, have you noticed ripple effects from a negative action?

_____

_____

_____

_____

_____

_____

_____

Friendship

3) For one week, strive to be especially kind to people. Call them by name. Make an extra effort to speak with them. Notice and appreciate their work. Journal how this makes you feel.

_____

_____

_____

_____

_____

_____

_____

_____

_____

_____

4) Return an act of meanness with an act of kindness. Make a conscious effort not to allow the mean act to change your mood or attitude. Note the reaction of the person who receives your kindness. Does the recipient change?

_____

_____

_____

_____

_____

_____

_____

Friendship

5) Make an anonymous act of kindness toward a person you will never meet. Journal about how this makes you feel.

_____

_____

_____

_____

_____

_____

_____

_____

_____

_____

_____

_____

_____

_____

_____

Friendship

Day 25
Think Happy Thoughts

The two women quickly walked to the end of the gym. Elizabeth balanced a long, plastic aerobics step on one hip as she took another drink from her sipper cup of water. Ellen dabbed her sweating face with a towel and glanced over at her friend.

"Okay, what's wrong? You haven't said one word during class and you never mess up like you did today."

Elizabeth shoved her step onto the storage rack. "I got a letter from my mother criticizing me, Paul came home for the third night in a row late, and Ryan got in trouble with his teacher. Other than that, life is hunky-dory. Unless you remember that I'm knee deep in the trade show preparations and have deadlines out the wazoo."

Ellen laughed. Only Elizabeth could combine hunky-dory and wazoo in three sentences. Her vocabulary was eclectic. It was Ellen's nature to see the humorous side, to be sunny and happy. Poor Elizabeth, however, seemed to have a little cloud permanently stationed over her head. Opposites must attract, she thought to herself, because Elizabeth is a great friend and I enjoy her even though our temperaments couldn't be more different. Goodness knows, if I'd had her parents I'd probably be a melancholy baby myself.

Friendship

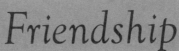

"Elizabeth, I have an idea. What if you started a club where you appointed designated worriers. One person could take acts of God, like hurricanes, droughts, tornados—"

Elizabeth caught the drift quickly, "And another could handle personal problems like divorces, quarrels, conflicts at work—"

"Then," added Ellen, "you could assign people a day a year to worry—"

"So that if a crisis occurs on your day, we know who to blame—"

"And that would free you up for the other 364 days a year," Ellen concluded as both women began to giggle.

"You crack me up," said Elizabeth. "You and your Pollyanna attitude are too much. Thank goodness you are my friend. Whatever will I do when you move away?" With that, both women became somber.

When Elizabeth arrived at work an hour later, a neat pile of printed papers sat in the tray of her fax machine. She rifled through them. One stood out. At the top was a huge cartoon of two women in exercise outfits. Beneath was this message: *Re: Happy thoughts. Clouds, cotton candy, hot chocolate, spring grass, and my daughter's hair. E*

That night before Elizabeth left the office, she faxed a message back to Ellen: *Re: Happy thoughts. Hazelnut coffee, Paul's cologne, Ryan's toothless grin, my space heater, clean towels at the gym. E*

Friendship

For months after that, the two women faxed or e-mailed or left messages on answering machines. When Ellen moved, the "happy thoughts" followed her to her new location. After the movers left, she opened the box she had carried with her in the car. She plugged in the fax and went about the business of unboxing her household items. A few hours later she passed by the fax machine. The paper in the tray read: Re: Happy thoughts. You. Me. Faxes. Forever friends. Love, *E.*

Friendship

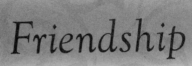

BLESSING

*Let me always turn my thoughts to the joys
life has to offer!*

1) Send an upbeat greeting to a friend. Journal about how you
felt about the greeting.

_____

_____

_____

_____

_____

_____

_____

2) Clip a cartoon from a newspaper and mail it to a person who
you think would appreciate it. Make a note of how you felt about
finding and sending the piece.

_____

_____

_____

_____

_____

_____

_____

_____

Friendship

3) Buy a few funny postcards and keep them handy. Send them to a friend along with a sincere compliment. How does it feel to appreciate your friend's good points?

_____

_____

_____

_____

_____

_____

_____

_____

_____

4) Respond to a co-worker's e-mail and add a sincere compliment. Write about what happens next.

_____

_____

_____

_____

_____

_____

_____

_____

_____

_____

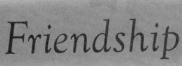

Friendship

5) Give a word of encouragement to someone you know is struggling. You may want to even tell a mother or father in the grocery store how well a child is behaving. How did he or she react?

_____

_____

_____

_____

_____

_____

_____

_____

_____

_____

_____

_____

_____

_____

_____

_____

_____

_____

_____

_____

_____

Yourself

Yourself

Day 26
Distinguish Reality from Fantasy

Cara was mad, mad, mad. On every front, life was falling apart.

The nonprofit board she had joined was becoming a colossal pain in the butt. The president had no leadership skills, and the monthly meetings degenerated from angry skirmishes to a disorganized waste of hours.

A bout with asthma had left her gasping so her exercise program had gone kaput. Around her waist, she felt as though she were carrying a belt of extra flesh. All her waistbands screamed at the added pressure, and Cara hated the way she looked.

The final blow struck when the carpool to her daughter's school collapsed. Cara's closest neighborhood friend had suddenly become unreliable, making calls at 9 p.m. the night before to say, "I'm driving Oliver from down the street to school tomorrow. His mother has an early appointment with her decorator. I guess you'll have to find another ride for Julie."

The three-day conference away from home couldn't have come at a worse time. As she dug through her closet, searching for outfits with elastic waistbands, the tears welled up in her eyes. Why did life have to be so hard?

Two days later, outside the hotel elevator, she heard someone call her name. "Cara? Cara is that you?" And Cara looked up into the

Yourself

face of Karen Lauder. Cara and Karen had met years ago at an earlier conference in Karen's home town. Karen had led the morning exercise program. Later, they discussed the difficulty of balancing career, children and a healthy life style. Now, Cara felt acutely conscious of every ounce she'd gained since their last meeting. She looked at Karen's slender waist and glowing face with a renewed sense of futility. Why? Why was life so hard?

Karen took her by the arm and led her away from the elevators. "What's wrong? I can see it in your face. This isn't the centered happy woman I've known for three years. What is it? Tell me!"

And it all came out. It blurted and burst and blew from Cara's mouth like a hurricane. Every bit of frustration about the exercise, the carpool, the board and more. A torrent of words swirled around them both. Then Karen reached over and pulled Cara into her arms.

"It's all choices, babe," and she quietly reminded Cara that she really did have control over her life. "Look to people whose lives are similar. Just because your carpool friend is another mom, doesn't mean her life is like yours. For example, I know two single mothers. One has family and a fairly straightforward job. Another has no nearby family, a hectic job and shared custody. Their lives are different, so their choices also have to be different. Look realistically over your life and then review your choices. Now, let me say a prayer for you."

And there, in the hallway of the hotel, she prayed over Cara.

The next week, Cara made some changes. She found a sitter to watch her daughter so that she could make up the work time she lost in picking her up from school. She called a doctor,

Yourself

picked up new asthma medicine, and signed up for that 6 a.m. exercise class she'd attended when she was in the best shape of her life. Then she tendered her resignation from the board.

There are many lives we could lead. But we'll never make the right choices for us until we give up the fantasy, dump the anger and look honestly at the life we really have.

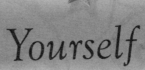

Yourself

BLESSING

The truth shall set you free! Being honest about your life gives you the clarity to make good choices.

1) Make yourself a chart covering all your waking hours in half-hour increments. Instead of scheduling your time, write down how you actually use your time.

6:30 am	_____
7 am	_____
7:30 am	_____
8 am	_____
8:30 am	_____
9 am	_____
9:30 am	_____
10 am	_____
10:30 am	_____
11 am	_____
11:30 am	_____
noon	_____
12:30 pm	_____
1 pm	_____
1:30 pm	_____
2 pm	_____
2:30 pm	_____
3 pm	_____

Yourself

3:30 pm _____

4 pm _____

4:30 pm _____

5 pm _____

5:30 pm _____

6 pm _____

6:30 pm _____

7 pm _____

7:30 pm _____

8 pm _____

8:30 pm _____

9 pm _____

9:30 pm _____

10 pm _____

10:30 pm _____

11 pm _____

6:30 am _____

7 am _____

7:30 am _____

8 am _____

8:30 am _____

9 am _____

9:30 am _____

10 am _____

10:30 am _____

Yourself

11 am	
11:30 am	
noon	
12:30 pm	
1 pm	
1:30 pm	
2 pm	
2:30 pm	
3 pm	
3:30 pm	
4 pm	
4:30 pm	
5 pm	
5:30 pm	
6 pm	
6:30 pm	
7 pm	
7:30 pm	
8 pm	
8:30 pm	
9 pm	
9:30 pm	
10 pm	
10:30 pm	
11 pm	

Yourself

2) How does this reality check match up with your fantasy about your life?

_____

_____

_____

_____

_____

_____

_____

_____

_____

_____

_____

3) Note three areas you'd like to change. Next to each area, note the smallest step you can take toward change. Commit to that smallest step.

CHANGE 1: _____

_____

_____

CHANGE 2: _____

_____

_____

CHANGE 3: _____

_____

_____

Yourself

4) Enlist the help of others. Do you have a problematic area of life? Ask a friend how he or she tackles this problem.

5) When you make a poor choice, write about that choice. Under what circumstances did you make the choice? What did you learn?

_____

_____

_____

_____

_____

_____

_____

_____

6) Select one fantasy area of your life and look at it realistically. If you always buy watermelon, but no one at your house eats it, quit buying watermelon. Journal about the change you make.

_____

_____

_____

_____

_____

_____

_____

_____

Yourself

Day 27
Buy Hyacinths to Feed Your Soul

"Look at that!" Marcia looked up from the ad she was writing to watch a bouquet of balloons move through the newspaper office. Over the tops of cubicles, the vibrant colors swayed like huge poppies. The balloons came closer and closer, until they stopped two rows away at the desk of another ad rep.

"Lucky stiff," said Lilly. Lilly and Marcia sat facing each other with only a low wall separating their work spaces. To Lilly's left was a gorgeous bouquet of red roses, a birthday bouquet from her husband.

"Right," mumbled Marcia, "like you've got room to complain."

When Marcia left the office at 5:15 p.m., she stopped to sniff Lilly's roses. Then she walked past the balloons. The last time someone had sent her flowers was when Dalton was born. Her husband, Greg, was in his own words, "not a flowers kind of guy." How did people attract other people who sent flowers? Hmmm. Seemed like a good question.

That weekend Marcia thought about flowers. As they pushed the Wal-Mart cart back into the corral, she asked, "Greg, why don't you buy me flowers?"

He looked mystified. "I guess 'cause I haven't done anything wrong," he said.

Yourself

He was, she reflected, a good man: a good father, a loving husband, and a steady wonderful mate. Although he never went wild on her birthdays, he always took her to dinner and brought her nice presents. On their anniversary, they went out to eat and usually to a movie. On Valentine's Day, he brought home mushy cards and a box of Whitman's chocolates. What Greg missed in flash, he made up for in day-in, day-out solicitude.

And still, she longed for flowers.

Monday morning Marcia dropped Dalton off at school and noticed the gas gauge had fallen to below a quarter of a tank. If she hurried, she could get gas on the way to work and still make it to their morning sales meeting on time. She impatiently fingered her charge card while waiting to check out. In front of her was one other patron, a mountain of a man at least 6'3" and weighing well over 200 pounds. His beard was salt and pepper, but neatly trimmed, and his boots were grey ostrich leather. On the counter he tossed a bag of pretzels, a carton of orange juice and a single yellow rose, he had selected from a bucket of flowers on display next to the cigarettes.

"For your sweetheart?" asked Marcia tentatively.

He blushed and gestured to the big Peterbilt truck idling right outside the door, "No, ma'am. For my cab."

Marcia stepped up to the cashier and hesitated. "The gas...and this..." And she gently laid a pink rose on the counter.

Yourself

BLESSING

*Today I will take responsibility for my own wants
and needs instead of waiting for others
to give me what I'd like.*

1) When was the last time you received flowers? Journal about that time.

_____

_____

_____

_____

_____

_____

_____

_____

2) Buy flowers for your home or office. How did you feel about making the purchase? How did you feel about having flowers?

_____

_____

_____

_____

_____

_____

_____

Yourself

3) Send flowers to a friend. What is the response?

_____

_____

_____

_____

_____

_____

_____

_____

4) Consider one everyday part of your life. How could you make it special? Write about your thoughts.

_____

_____

_____

_____

_____

_____

_____

_____

_____

_____

_____

_____

Yourself

5) Do you easily spend money on yourself? If you don't, why don't you? Write about how it feels to make a luxury purchase for yourself.

_____

_____

_____

_____

_____

_____

_____

_____

_____

_____

_____

_____

_____

_____

_____

_____

_____

_____

_____

_____

Yourself

Day 28
No Regrets

"**D**o you ever regret that you have only one child? I mean with Colleen being so sick and all..." The woman's voice trailed off.

Deanna Wilson pulled back the plaid napkins that surrounded the breadsticks. There was only one left. She took it and tore off a small chunk which she put in her mouth and chewed thoughtfully.

Regret? Regret that there was only Colleen?

"No, I never have," she said firmly.

On that sleeting March day in the doctor's office when he said, "It's Hodgkin's disease," she was glad there was only Colleen. That way, Deanna could turn her entire attention to the situation at hand. Was it fatal? What did it mean? What must they do next?

Because there was only Colleen, Deanna didn't have to worry about picking up another child after volleyball practice. Because there was only Colleen, Deanna had only to call Avery and ask him to meet them immediately at the doctor's office. Deanna was free to hold her daughter and cry and not try to be strong for anyone's sake.

Later, she could accompany Colleen to the hospital for the treatments. She could hold her daughter's head as she vomited, endlessly it seemed. She could help Colleen into the starchy white sheets of the hospital bed and hold her hand for hours until Colleen fell into an exhausted sleep.

Yourself

Because there was just Colleen, Deanna could plan for small treats like buying a quart of Col's favorite ice cream and never worry that another child might want exactly that flavor and that Colleen might have to share. Since Colleen was an only child, Deanna didn't worry about the time or money they spent on all the bills that accompanied illnesses, the bills Avery then fought the insurance company about for months.

With only Colleen to care for, Deanna could sit beside her daughter all night. They could talk and giggle and plan a future that might never, ever happen. Deanna could fall asleep on the floor and not worry about conserving her energy to help another child. With just one, with that only precious daughter, Deanna was free to give her all to her child.

At one point, knowing Colleen might die, Deanna did wonder, "How will I live without being a mother?" But she also realized, with brutal honesty, that with one child she had been a ten on the motherhood scale, and with two or more, she might only have been a five or six. Colleen might leave this earth prematurely, but she would leave it having had the best childhood her mother could possibly give.

"I have no regrets," said Deanna again. "I have enjoyed every moment of being Colleen's mother. I couldn't ask for more." Then, she decided she couldn't eat another bite.

Yourself

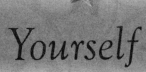

BLESSING

Thank you for the ability to honestly appraise a situation and enjoy it. What works for me, might not work for other people. Help me always to be honest with myself about what is good for me.

1) Consider an area of your life that is non-traditional. How is it different from the norm? Write about it.

_____

_____

_____

_____

_____

_____

_____

2) Think about an area of your life you'd like to change. Does the weight of other's opinions hold you back? Journal your thoughts.

_____

_____

_____

_____

_____

_____

_____

Yourself

3) Think up a wild dream. Day dream about a change you'd like to make. How wild is that dream? What stops you from making the change? Is there any part of the change you might embrace? Write down your thoughts.

_____

_____

_____

_____

_____

_____

_____

_____

_____

_____

4) What works for you that might not—and probably doesn't— work for other people. Write about that area of your life.

_____

_____

_____

_____

_____

_____

_____

_____

_____

Yourself

5) *Is there any part of your life that causes other people to feel surprise? If so, what is that area and how do you feel about it? Write your response.*

_____

_____

_____

_____

_____

_____

_____

_____

_____

_____

_____

_____

_____

_____

_____

_____

_____

Yourself

Day 29
One a Day

" I don't see how you do it," the voice on the other end of the car phone said. "Glenna, you have the busiest schedule of anyone I know. And you still manage to get it all done. But when do you ever just sit?"

Glenna frowned and accelerated around a truck blocking her path.

"I don't," she said cheerfully.

No doubt about it, Glenna MacAvoy had a full schedule. Up at 5:30 a.m. to exercise, at her job by 7:30 a.m., done at 3 p.m. to pick up the children from school, and dinner on the table at 5:30 p.m. so that when Walt MacAvoy walked through the door he walked into a scene worthy of a Norman Rockwell painting. Three adorable kids sat in their places at the kitchen table. His lovely, slim wife greeted him with a kiss. He set down his briefcase, slid into his seat, and led the family in prayer.

No time to waste was her motto. Idle hands are the devil's playthings, her grandmother had taught her. Being organized was the key.

Underwear was rotated in the drawers so that each pair received equal wear. No pets allowed because animals dirty up the house. New magazines went in the magazine rack and old ones came out. Library book due dates were marked in red on the calendar

in the kitchen. Each child—Beth, Bobbie, and Becky—had his/her own backpack and a colored folder for bringing home notes from school.

Glenna's morning walk was all the exercise she needed. It took her precisely 45 minutes to walk from the MacAvoy's house to the small park on the other side of the neighborhood. To keep on schedule, Glenna walked at a quick clip, ignoring the benches scattered along the park's edge. With spring coming, the tips of the trees were touched with soft green buds. Glenna noticed, but she did not slow her pace.

And so it went until one morning when Glenna was adjusting the dial on her car radio. She always checked the weather and the traffic report at precisely 7:21 a.m. Today, her finger hit the wrong button, and she found herself listening to the public radio station. Traffic was heavy. She couldn't reach down to change the station. The minor change in her schedule irritated her, but there was nothing she could do.

"You are the oldest woman in the county," said the interviewer, "In fact, you turn 104 this weekend, Mrs. Simmons. What keeps you going?"

A whispy voice floated from the dashboard, "Why I take the time to smell the roses, young man. We are not human *doings*. We're human *beings*. What a sin it is to hustle and bustle through life not enjoying one bit of it. I wake up every day excited about the sunrise! You only get one a day you know."

Glenna pulled into her parking place at work and turned off the car. For a moment she sat still. When was the last time she had seen a sunrise? She walked through them every day, but honestly, she couldn't remember looking up.

Yourself

At dinner that night she concentrated on the faces of her children. When was the last time she really, really looked at them. Becky's face was lengthening and looking more like her father's every day. Bobbie's babyish curls were relaxing as he grew older. Soon his hair would only have a hint of a wave, no sign of the unruly mop he'd had as a toddler. And Beth, her baby, now stood shoulder high to Glenna. Where had the time gone?

The next morning, Glenna walked briskly past the first bench, the second, and the third. But with each footfall, a force seemed to pull at her. Finally, she turned. Slowly, she walked to a bench. Slowly, she sat down. The sky was streaked with gold and orange as the sun came over the tree tops.

Back at the house, Walt was setting out vitamins at each place setting. Becky poured the orange juice, and Bobby piled toast onto a plate. Beth greeted her mother with a hug.

"You only get one a day," echoed a voice in Glenna's mind. "Only one a day."

Yourself

BLESSING

Slow me down. Let me make the time to
enjoy life instead of hurrying past it.

1) When was the last time you slowed down? Took a nap? Watched a sunset or sunrise? Looked for a four-leaf clover? Write about that time.

_____

_____

_____

_____

_____

_____

_____

_____

_____

_____

_____

2) Who is most likely to encourage you to take time for yourself? Make a note of that person and how you feel about him or her.

_____

_____

_____

_____

_____

Yourself

3) *If you had no one on earth to please but yourself, how might you live your daily life differently? Write your thoughts.*

_____

_____

_____

_____

_____

_____

_____

_____

_____

_____

4) *When was the last time you sat and talked to the people you love? Take time. Ask them how they are enjoying life. Their answers will be enlightening. Journal them.*

_____

_____

_____

_____

_____

_____

_____

_____

_____

_____

_____

Yourself

5) Sit quietly outside for a while. How long were you able to sit? What did you hear? What did you see? What did you smell? Write about the experience.

_____
_____
_____
_____
_____
_____
_____
_____
_____
_____
_____
_____
_____
_____
_____
_____
_____

Yourself

Day 30
It Would Take a Lifetime to Do All This

"Slowly, slowly..."

Roxanne walked her side of the hot air balloon gently toward the pilot as he rocked the gondola, the enormous wicker basket, into an upright position. The whoosh of the flame as the lit propane gas surged from the nozzle in his hands caused the balloon crew to jump. Roxanne paused as she walked and glanced back over her shoulder to see the beautiful colors of the balloon as it filled with hot air. From her vantage point, the interior of the balloon looked like a humongous stained glass window.

They finished righting the balloon. Roxanne stood to one side and watched as the attendants helped the first nursing home resident toddle slowly towards the balloon. With great care, the attendants lifted the stiff woman into the gondola. Her face blossomed with joy. The balloon crew solemnly let out the tether, hand over hand. Within minutes, the huge balloon floated serenely above the Crystal Lake Home for the Aged. With the tether holding the balloon securely to a van, they could give people balloon "rides" for hours.

Roxanne hummed to herself as she helped haul in the balloon, hand over hand. The elderly woman was lifted out of the basket, and the next resident stepped forward, eager as a small child.

Yourself

Six people took rides before the group began to chant, "Dudley, Dudley, Dudley." From behind the wheelchairs, a thin figure began to hobble forward on a silver, four-legged walker. He stopped and waved at the crowd, then resumed his snail-like pace.

At the gondola, the attendants had to hold Dudley in an almost horizontal position to slide him into the basket. He was so stiff that his body could not bend and his legs could not step up off the ground.

"You old fool! Dudley! You're crazy, Dud!" shouted a few quavering voices. Dudley's smile never faded. His eyes were bright as twinkling Christmas tree lights.

Once aloft in the gondola, Dudley turned slowly, slowly around to appreciate the view from all sides. He waved. He waved again. Then he turned another time.

The attendants repeated the same tortuous process in reverse to lift and levitate the stiff man out of the gondola. They settled Dudley on the ground and got his hands up onto the walker. Roxanne's position had been relieved by another hot air balloon crew member, so she walked over to where the old man was standing. With great effort she saw him reach into his back pocket of his pants and pull out a tiny red notebook. Tucked into the wire spiral binding was the stub of a yellow #2 pencil. Dudley licked the pencil point and struck through something written in the notebook. He slid the pencil back into the wire and started to return the notebook when it dropped from his hand onto the ground.

Yourself

Roxanne stepped through the crowd quickly. "I'll get it," she told the old man. As she picked up the notebook, she saw what was written in it. Page after page listed "Things to Do." A fresh strike-through had marked out "Ride in a Hot Air Balloon." On the same page had been written: "See Notre Dame's football team play. Take a tour of the inside of the White House. Eat snails."

Dudley was an optimist. At the bottom of the page he'd scribbled, "Date Sophia Loren."

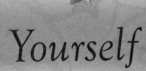

Yourself

BLESSING

This world offers me so much to see and do.
Thank you for the endless variety of activities,
places and people I can enjoy.

1) Use an inexpensive notebook to create a wish list. Start by
writing some of your life goals.

GOAL: _____

_____

_____

GOAL: _____

_____

_____

GOAL: _____

_____

_____

GOAL: _____

_____

_____

GOAL: _____

_____

_____

GOAL: _____

_____

_____

Yourself

2) Add photos of places you'd like to visit. Listen to a travel program on television or radio and add new places.

❑ _____
❑ _____
❑ _____
❑ _____
❑ _____
❑ _____
❑ _____
❑ _____
❑ _____
❑ _____
❑ _____

3) Get your passport or renew it. How does it feel to have a passport? You may wish to view the movie Breaking Away for a perspective on passport ownership.

_____
_____
_____
_____
_____
_____
_____
_____
_____

Yourself

4) In your notebook, write adventures you'd like to have. Number the adventures. They don't have to be big or wild.

_____

_____

_____

_____

_____

_____

_____

_____

_____

_____

_____

5) What commonplace activities have you missed? The other day a friend told me she'd never been to a football game. What is commonplace for others that you've never done? What is holding you back? Write about your feelings.

_____

_____

_____

_____

_____

_____

_____

_____

_____

Bonus

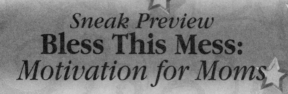

Bless This Mess:
Motivation for Moms

The Great Grape
Adventure

While walking to the kitchen, I noticed the small portable vacuum cleaner sitting in the center of the living room carpet. Its cord stretched from the socket across the room. No boys were in sight. For a quick moment, I wondered what was going on. Then the timer went off in the kitchen and I hurried to turn over the chicken nuggets baking in the oven.

When I turned around, I noticed a box of Tide sitting on the kitchen island. In the sink was a crumpled rag. By the side of the sink was a tiny trickle of purple.

I called the boys up from the basement.

"What's going on?" I asked. They looked at each other. They looked at me. They looked at their feet. Then they mumbled, "Nothing."

"Why is the vacuum cleaner in the middle of the living room floor?" I persisted.

"We were just cleaning up," ventured Michael. And then, he broke. He began to jabber like a blue jay near a bird feeder. "And it was Joon Ho's fault and I told him not to and he told me not to tell and I think we got it all up."

Joon Ho was violently shaking his head at this point. "Not my fault! Not my fault!"

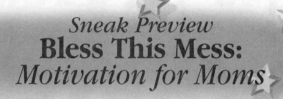

Sneak Preview
Bless This Mess:
Motivation for Moms

I never did figure out whose fault it was. I didn't care. The rule was **no eating outside of the kitchen.** The problem was purple grape juice spilled in the living room on my white carpet and white brocade sofa. Of all the food choices they could have made, the boys decided on the one liquid most likely to leave a permanent stain.

Miraculously, the boys had managed to get up the majority of the color. Dissolving a small amount of Tide in water, they had made a cleaning liquid and attacked the dribble with a great deal of effort. Most of the purple had come out. But, there will always be a light violet shadow on the sofa and the carpet. Unless we recarpet or recover our sofa, that stain is permanent.

After the boys were in bed that night, the representatives from their school called. In three short months, Joon Ho would be returning to Korea. A snag in the visa process was to take him home to his parents six months earlier than we had all planned. Over the time of Joon Ho's stay, Michael had become dependent on his new "brother." In the months we'd spent together, Joon Ho had—on occasion—called me "Mom." We hadn't planned to say goodbye so quickly, and yet we would do so.

I sat down on the sofa to think. Outside the stars twinkled gently over our lawn. The dog came and lay down at my feet with a sigh. The whole house had become quiet. Then the moon shifted from behind a cloud and filled the room with brightness. I looked down and saw the stain. In the dim light, it was barely visible, almost like it never happened. There was only a faint reminder. Somehow, I was glad it was there.

Bless This Mess:
Motivation for Moms

BLESSING

Help me to focus on what matters. Let us all leave our traces behind so that we never forget those we love.

1) Think of a stain you have on some item. How did it get there? Does it tell a story?

_____

_____

_____

_____

_____

_____

_____

_____

2) Think of some mark you may leave behind. What might that mark look like?

_____

_____

_____

_____

_____

_____

_____

_____

_____

3) How do you remember others who have moved out of your life?

_____

_____

_____

_____

_____

_____

_____

_____

_____

4) Consider an item you owned that has been ruined. How did you feel about it being ruined? Why do you consider it ruined? (Was anything really ruined, or had your perspective just changed?)

_____

_____

_____

_____

_____

_____

_____

_____

Sneak Preview
Bless This Mess:
Motivation for Moms

5) How might you create touchstones to remind you of those you love? Create a list of ways.

❏ _____

_____

❏ _____

_____

❏ _____

_____

❏ _____

_____

❏ _____

_____

❏ _____

_____

❏ _____

_____

❏ _____

_____

❏ _____

_____

Bonus

NOTES & THOUGHTS

Bonus

NOTES & THOUGHTS

Bonus

NOTES & THOUGHTS

More from Joanna

ISBN: 0-9630222-8-8
128 pages (1999) $19.99

Scrapbook Storytelling

Save family stories and memories with photos, journaling and your own creativity.

Learn how to document stories—from a quick sentence to page after scrapbook page. The book is full of ways to recover stories from the past, discover the stories in the present and create stories that light the path to the future.

With easy to understand steps for documenting stories, readers can choose to combine narrative with photos, journals, memorabilia and more.

ISBN: 0-930500-02-5
80 pages (2001) $14.99

Quick & Easy Pages

Save more memories in less time.

If you've ever wished you had more time to scrapbook, or didn't think you had the time to start, this is the book for you. Joanna shares easy ways to present photographs and pull together pages. You'll learn over a hundred speedy scrapbooking techniques along with dozens of money-saving tips. Great how-to photos guide you through each step.